WHITEWORK
EMBROIDERY

STACKPOLE BOOKS

An imprint of Globe Pequot

Trade Division of The Rowman & Littlefield Publishing Group, Inc.

4501 Forbes Blvd., Ste. 200

Lanham, MD 20706

www.stackpolebooks.com

Distributed by NATIONAL BOOK NETWORK

SHIROI ITO NO SHISHU (NV70398)

Copyright © 2017 by Ayako Otsuka/NIHON VOGUE-SHA.

All rights reserved. Original Japanese edition published by Nihon Vogue Co.

English language licensed by World Book Media, LLC.

Email: info@worldbookmedia.com

Photography by Kato Shinsaku and Shirai Yukari

We have made every effort to ensure the accuracy and completeness of
these instructions. We cannot, however, be responsible for human error,
typographical mistakes, or variations in individual work.

British Library Cataloguing in Publication Information available

Library of Congress Cataloging-in-Publication Data available

ISBN 978-0-8117-3822-4 (paperback)
ISBN 978-0-8117-6823-8 (e-book)

Translator: Kyoko Matthews
English Editor: Lindsay Fair
Technical Editor: Yvette Stanton
Page design and layout: Arati Devasher, aratidevasher.com

First Edition

Printed in China

WHITEWORK EMBROIDERY

Learn the Stitches plus 30 Step-by-Step Projects

AYAKO OTSUKA

Contents

Introduction

Embroidery is common among nearly every civilization in history, with each culture possessing its own unique styles and methods. Long before the development of advanced dyeing and weaving technology, embroidery provided a way to embellish textiles designated for special occasions.

During medieval times, embroidered textiles were reserved for royalty and the church. In contrast to the heavily embroidered designs featuring richly colored silk and even metallic threads, there also developed a more delicate style of embroidery worked exclusively in white. Known as *opus teutonicum*, white linen thread was used to embroider white linen cloth to create altar coverings in 12th century Europe, particularly in the areas that would eventually become Germany. This is considered to be one of the earliest forms of whitework.

By the 16th and 17th centuries, whitework embroidery was no longer reserved for church vestments, but could also be seen on women's clothing and household linens. New techniques emerged, including open work, cut work, and needlelace.

As the world's leading producer of linen, Europe became known for whitework embroidery. Over time, different regions developed their own styles, such as Hedebo in Denmark and Schwalm in Germany. In fact, there are so many different whitework styles and techniques that it's impossible to include them all in this book. Instead, I've included five different whitework techniques. Let's start by learning a bit more about each of these techniques.

Schwalm Embroidery

Schwalm embroidery originated in Germany and incorporates many different whitework techniques. Schwalm embroidery designs were inspired by the Tree of Life and feature flowers, leaves, hearts, and birds. Schwalm embroidery closely resembles the Hvidsøm style of Hedebo. One way to tell the two styles apart is to examine the rows of stitching surrounding the designs: Hvidsøm often features two rows of chain stitch, while Schwalm often features a drawn thread motif surrounded by one row of chain stitch and one row of coral knots, with the potential for more rows of decorative stitching.

Hedebo Embroidery

Hedebo is a style of whitework that originated in the farming communities of the Hedebo, or heathland, region of Denmark. As Hedebo embroidery maintained popularity for a span of nearly 200 years, several different styles developed. One of the most common styles is Hedebo needlelace, where shapes are constructed, then filled with patterns of pyramids, bars, and rings made using the buttonhole stitch. The patterned shapes can be cut and stitched directly into a piece of fabric or can be attached as an edge. Another style of Hedebo embroidery used in this book is Hvidsøm, which features drawn thread work motifs surrounded by rows of chain stitch.

Drawn Thread Work

Drawn thread work is an open work embroidery technique in which threads are cut and removed from a piece of fabric, then the remaining threads are grouped together to create patterns. This technique often utilizes hemstitching to create decorative borders along the edges of linens, clothing, and samplers.

Counted Thread Work

Counted thread embroidery is a general term for any embroidery in which the fabric threads are counted as you stitch, such as cross-stitch or needlepoint. A couple of the projects in this book use a counted thread work technique commonly used in the early styles of Hedebo, where satin stitches are made over counted fabric threads to produce geometric patterns.

Pulled Thread Work

Pulled thread work is an open work embroidery technique that does not involve cutting and removing fabric threads. Instead, tension is applied when working the stitches to pull the fabric threads together, producing a lacy effect. One of the unique characteristics of this technique is that the stitches themselves are not meant to be visible—matching thread and fabric are used to produce the open work effect. This technique was particularly popular in 18th century Germany, where Dresden work became a substitute for expensive lace.

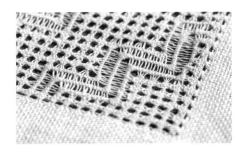

Whitework Sampler I

If you're new to whitework or simply need a refresher, this sampler is an ideal place to start. Samplers allow you to practice stitching techniques before tackling a complex project. Once complete, you'll have a beautiful wall hanging to display!

Techniques:
Schwalm Embroidery (a-i)
Hedebo Embroidery (j-m)
Drawn Thread Work (n-s)
Broderie Anglaise (t)
Counted Thread Work (u)
Hvidsøm Embroidery (v-x)

Instructions on page 88

Quatrefoil Doily

This lovely doily is created by stitching the same motif four times. Repetitive patterns can be quite striking with their symmetry—just make sure the combination of stitches is interesting to ensure good design. **Techniques: Hedebo Embroidery (j-l) and Broderie Anglaise (t)**

Instructions on page 92

Edgework Dish Covers

Use linen dish covers to store and protect valuable plates. Simple edge motifs created with Hedebo embroidery techniques add a pretty touch.

Techniques: Hedebo Embroidery (j and k)

Instructions on page 94

Teapot Cozy

Make teatime a special event with this beautifully embroidered teapot cozy. The finished product may look quite elaborate, but the design is composed of basic stitches. **Techniques: Hedebo Embroidery (j-m) and Broderie Anglaise (t)**

Instructions on page 96

To create the teapot cozy, you'll stitch up a separate front and back, and then connect the pieces using buttonhole scallops. When working with Hedebo, it's important to achieve balance among the open work portions of the design. Use ladder stitch, pyramids, and buttonhole scallops to fill the cut areas, and then add thick satin stitches to provide weight and contrast.

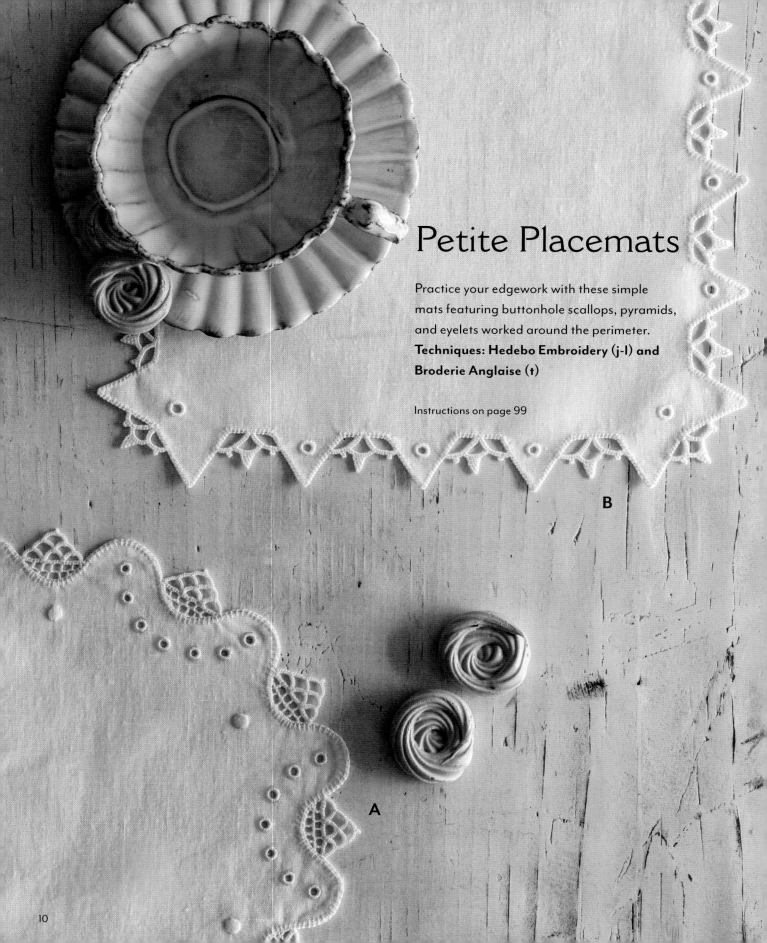

Petite Placemats

Practice your edgework with these simple mats featuring buttonhole scallops, pyramids, and eyelets worked around the perimeter.
Techniques: Hedebo Embroidery (j-l) and Broderie Anglaise (t)

Instructions on page 99

B

A

Buttonhole Scallop Coasters

These small coasters can be stitched up quickly, making for a perfect gift to celebrate a friend's housewarming. Work Hedebo buttonhole stitch around the edge of the linen fabric, then add pretty scallops at the corners for a special touch. You can even experiment with color to create a one-of-a-kind set. **Technique: Hedebo Embroidery (j)**

Instructions on page 149

The Cushion Collection

On the following pages, you'll find seven unique pillow designs incorporating a variety of whitework techniques. You'll discover all sorts of shapes, from classic squares to cylindrical bolster pillows, plus an assortment of embroidery motifs to suit your personal style.

Floral Cushion

This symmetrical floral design features several classic elements of Schwalm embroidery and will add an elegant touch to any room. **Techniques: Schwalm Embroidery (b-e, g, and h)**

Instructions on page 102

Snowflake Cushion

Despite its complex appearance, this geometric pattern is mostly composed of straight stitches done using counted thread work. Bands of four-sided stitch frame this Scandinavian-inspired design. **Techniques: Drawn Thread Work (n) and Counted Thread Work (u)**

Instructions on page 104

Teddy Bear Pillow

Use Schwalm embroidery to stitch up this sweet design. Different stitches are used for the various parts of the bear in order to create dimension and texture within the motif.
Techniques: Schwalm Embroidery (a, c, d, f, and i) and Drawn Thread Work (n, q, r,and s)

Instructions on page 106

Hen Pillow

Perfect for life in the country, this cute and quirky design features a friendly fowl created with pulled thread work. A triangular Hardanger-style edge motif is attached along the top and bottom edges of the pillow for a playful look. **Techniques: Pulled Thread Embroidery (A-J)**

Instructions on page 108

Drawn Thread Bolster & Broderie Anglaise Cushion

Make any bed, sofa, or chair more inviting with these uniquely shaped cushions. The pretty cylindrical pillow is created with simple drawn work and dainty flowers, while the round pillow features gorgeous eyelets and soft ruffles. Both designs utilize heavy satin stitch motifs to balance out the empty spaces created by the removal of threads. **Techniques: Hedebo Embroidery (m), Drawn Thread Work (o), and Broderie Anglaise (t)**

Instructions on pages 110 and 112

Envelope Pillow

Delicate Hedebo motifs embellish the flap of this ingeniously constructed pillow. The embroidery pattern may appear rather intricate, but it's composed of simple stitches, so it's not as hard as it looks! **Techniques: Hedebo Embroidery (j–l) and Broderie Anglaise (t)**

Instructions on page 114

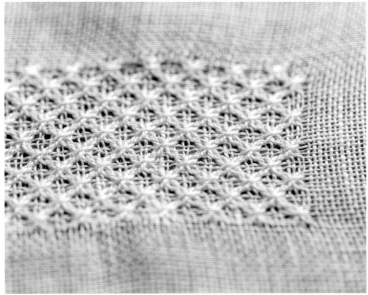

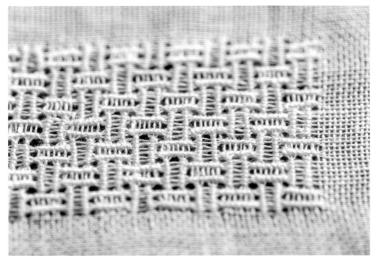

Whitework Sampler II

Pulled thread work allows you to create intricate open work patterns without removing a single thread. Instead, stitches are used to manipulate the fabric threads in order to create a variety of designs, as illustrated by this sampler.

Technique: Pulled Thread Embroidery

A: Wrapped stitch

B: Chessboard filling stitch

C: Checker filling stitch

D: Step stitch

E: Wave stitch

F: Greek cross filling stitch

G: Wrapped stitch + four-sided stitch

H: Cable stitch

I: Ringed backstitch

J: Step stitch + four-sided stitch

Instructions on page 116

Christening Gown

This traditional dress makes a special baby gift that's sure to become a family heirloom for years to come. Combine satin and outline stitches with Hedebo embroidery to embellish the gown with beautiful floral motifs. **Techniques: Hedebo Embroidery (j-m) and Broderie Anglaise (t)**

Instructions on page 119

Techniques: Hedebo
Embroidery (j and
l) and Broderie
Anglaise (t)
Instructions on page 132

Bundle of Joy Layette

Celebrate the arrival of a new baby with this stunning set. Each piece features
a sprawling foliage and floral motif to symbolize life and growth.

Techniques: Hedebo Embroidery (j and m) and Brøderie Anglaise (t)
Instructions on page 126

Techniques: Hedebo Embroidery (k and l) and Brøderie Anglaise (t)
Instructions on page 129

25

Scented Sachets

Fill these cute little sachets with your favorite dried herbs, then tuck inside a drawer or closet to perfume your clothes and linens with the most incredible scents. The flap-style designs can also be used as small pouches. **Techniques: Hedebo Embroidery (j-l) and Broderie Anglaise (t)**

Instructions on page 134

Drawstring Pouches

A circular bottom and drawstring closure provide these adorable pouches with a playful, puffy shape, while semicircular buttonhole scallop edging complements the round silhouette. Experiment with colored fabric and thread to change the look of this design. **Technique: Hedebo Embroidery (j)**

Instructions on page 138

Ring Bearer Pillow

As symbols of love and commitment, wedding rings deserve a place of honor during the ceremony. This beautiful square cushion features a Hvidsøm floral design and even includes special ribbon holders for the rings. After the ceremony, the cushion will serve as a meaningful keepsake that the bride and groom will cherish forever. **Techniques: Hedebo Embroidery (j) and Hvidsøm Embroidery (v-x)**

Instructions on page 140

Everyday Table Runner

This simple pulled thread work table runner is designed to withstand the rigors of everyday life. Since the threads aren't actually removed, the linen is surprisingly strong, despite its delicate lace pattern. **Technique: Pulled Thread Embroidery (J)**

Instructions on page 144

Modern Napkin Rings

Featuring just a single stitch, these napkin rings are casual enough for daily use. The four-sided stitch really pops when worked on contrasting gray linen. **Technique: Drawn Thread Work (n)**

Instructions on page 137

Embroidery Tool Case

This tool caddy features the same embroidery motif as the Snowflake Cushion on page 15, but creates a different impression when worked on gray linen. Constructed using the counted thread work technique, the style is similar to Japanese koginzashi embroidery. **Techniques: Drawn Thread Work (n) and Counted Thread Work (u)**

Instructions on page 146

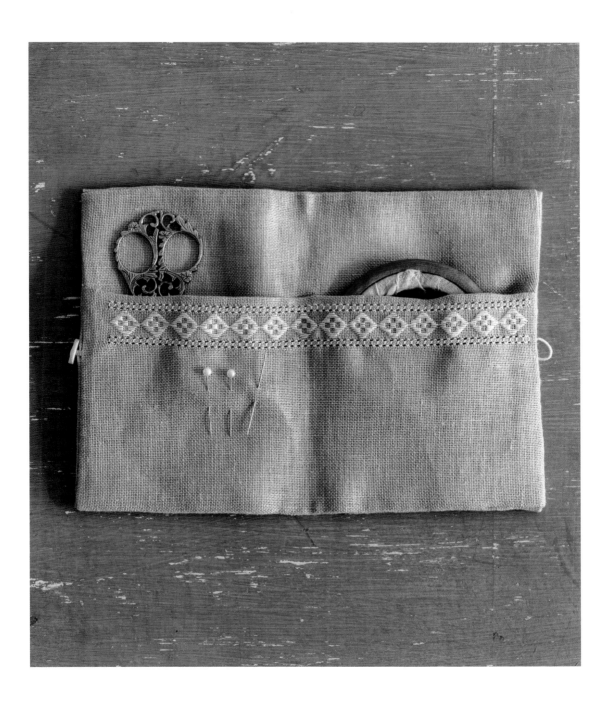

Cube Pincushions & Needle Book

These small projects are great for beginners, or a nice option if you need to take a break from a more complicated design. Buttonhole scallops and pyramids combine to create decorative edgings on these boxy pincushions and coordinating needle book. **Techniques: Hedebo Embroidery (j and k)**

Instructions on pages 150 and 151

Pincushion

This unique design features different stitches on each of its four corners. Use it as a miniature sampler to practice your stitch work, then add it to a basic pincushion for a special touch. Though this sampler may be small, it contains all the charm Hedebo embroidery has to offer. **Techniques: Hedebo Embroidery (j-l) and Broderie Anglaise (t)**

Instructions on page 152

Tools & Materials

You'll need basic embroidery supplies to stitch the designs in this book. The following guide explains what to look for when selecting tools and materials for whitework.

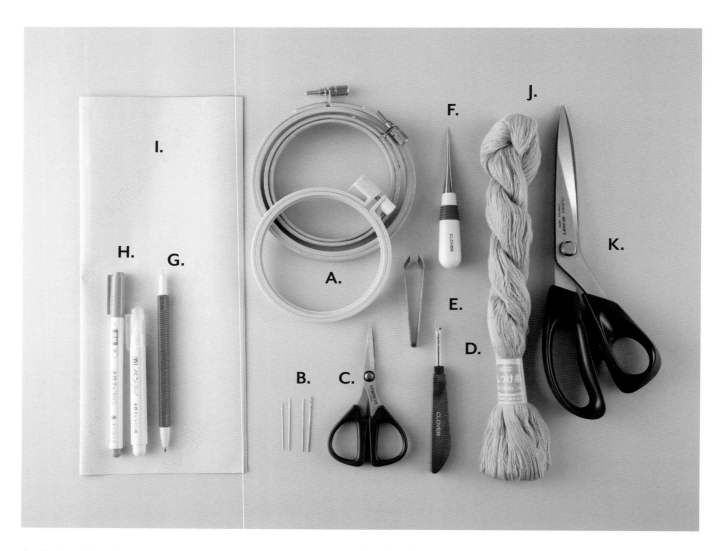

A. Embroidery hoops

A 4–6 in (10–15 cm) hoop works well for most of the designs in this book—just move the hoop as you work on different areas. The fabric should be drum-tight within the hoop. When you stretch the fabric, ensure you only pull with the fabric grain and not on the bias.

B. Needles

Use a needle that suits the stitch and the thickness of the thread. Use an embroidery needle with a sharp point for Hedebo or outlines of Schwalm embroidery, which uses finely woven fabric. Use a blunt-ended tapestry needle for filling stitches of Schwalm embroidery, drawn thread work, counted thread work, and pulled thread work. See page 37 for more information about needles recommended for whitework.

C. Embroidery scissors

Choose good quality scissors with sharp, finely pointed blades.

D. Seam ripper

Use to cut and remove woven threads for drawn work.

E. Tweezers

When withdrawing threads, tweezers can grab what fingers cannot. They are very helpful for Schwalm and drawn work.

F. Awl

Useful for making eyelet holes.

G. Stylus

Use in conjunction with carbon chalk paper to transfer the embroidery design onto fabric. You can purchase a special tool or use an empty pen.

H. Transfer pens

Use to mark fabric and transfer embroidery designs. Most transfer pens are water soluble, which means their marks can be erased with a damp cloth, while some require a corresponding eraser pen.

I. Carbon chalk paper

Specifically designed for crafting, this special chalk paper is used to transfer designs onto fabric. Place the paper chalk side down against the fabric. Position the embroidery design on top and trace using a stylus. The pressure from the stylus will transfer the outline of the design onto the fabric.

J. Basting thread

Baste around the edges of your fabric before embroidering to prevent fraying

K. Fabric scissors

Designate a pair of sharp scissors exclusively for use cutting fabric.

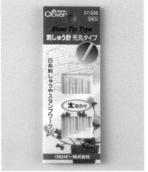

Needles

Choose your needle according to the thread thickness, fabric thickness, and stitches you'll be working. The needle shaft should be the same thickness as the doubled thread (because it comes out each side of the eye, making a double thickness).

Use sharp-pointed needles for Hedebo and the surrounding stitches of Schwalm embroidery motifs. Use blunt tapestry needles for techniques that require you to count the fabric threads, such as drawn thread work, pulled thread work, and counted thread work—this will prevent the fabric threads from splitting as you stitch.

I recommend Clover brand needles because they glide through the fabric smoothly and do not break easily.

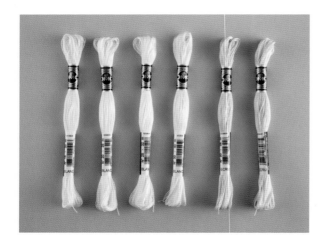

Thread

DMC Coton a Broder was used for most of the projects in this book. Coton a broder is a non-divisible thread composed of five loosely twisted plies. This thread is available in multiple thicknesses, including: #16, #20, #25, and #30. You'll see these numbers noted next to the stitch names within the embroidery motifs. Just like needle sizes, the larger the number, the thinner the thread. Typically, thicker threads are used with coarse fabrics, while thinner threads are used with finely woven fabrics, but some projects utilize multiple weights of thread for the different design elements, such as thicker thread for outside borders and thinner thread for needlelace.

To use coton a broder, pull a 24–28 in (60–70 cm) long piece from the skein, cut it, and thread your needle—there are no strands to separate, so you can start stitching right away. Use one strand when stitching with coton a broder.

Some of the projects also use other types of thread, such as DMC six-strand embroidery floss and pearl cotton.

A selection of the fabrics used in this book: From left to right, 28 count, 30 count (in both white and gray), 32 count, 38 count, 45 count, and 55 count (in both blue and white).

Fabric

Whitework is traditionally stitched on linen fabric. Look for high-quality evenweave fabric, which is fabric woven with the same number of warp (vertical) and weft (horizontal) threads per inch. Evenweave fabric is available in various counts, which represent the number of threads per inch in either direction. For example, 28 count fabric has 28 threads per inch across both the warp and weft of the fabric.

Lower count fabrics are suitable for beginners because they're easier to see and count, while higher count fabrics will produce fine embroidery work. The projects in this book are stitched on fabric ranging from 28 to 55 count. Schwalm embroidery, drawn thread work, pulled thread work, and counted thread work are all counted embroideries where you must position the stitches by counting the fabric threads. Choose a count where you can see the individual threads well enough to count them.

Note that about 6 in (15 cm) extra fabric has been included in the material requirements for each project. This extra fabric will allow the work to fit nicely in a hoop, making the embroidery process easier.

Schwalm Embroidery

Schwalm embroidery motifs require removing some of the fabric threads to make a base on which to stitch. In order to prevent the fabric from destabilizing, stitch around the design to make a border, then remove some of the fabric threads within the shape in preparation for the filling stitches.

Stitch the Motif Border

The first step in stitching Schwalm embroidery motifs is to sew the motif border, which will form a stable outline for the drawn thread work. With Schwalm embroidery, the motif borders are typically composed of one row of coral stitch and one row of chain stitch. Use a sharp-pointed needle to stitch this part of the motif.

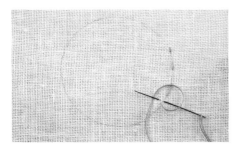

1. First, work running stitch along part of the motif outline to secure the thread. To start the coral stitch, take a short stitch across the line so the needle points toward the center. Take the thread under the needle point in a counterclockwise direction.

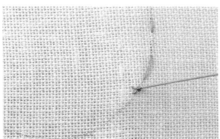

2. Pull the thread to tighten the stitch. One coral stitch is complete.

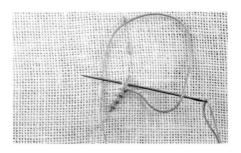

3. Continue making coral stitches along the motif outline, working in a counterclockwise direction. The coral stitches will hide the running stitches made in step 1.

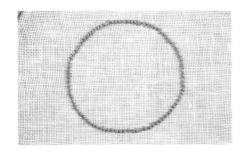

4. Once the entire circle of coral stitch is complete, finish the thread by running it under a few stitches on the wrong side of the fabric.

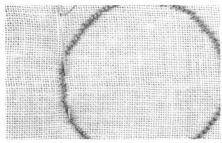

5. Next, you'll work a circle of chain stitch along the inside edge of the coral stitch. Secure the thread by working running stitch before you begin chain stitch.

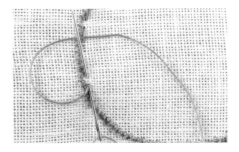

6. To make the first chain stitch, insert the needle in the same hole as where the thread emerged in step 5. Bring it out a short distance along. Take the thread under the needle point.

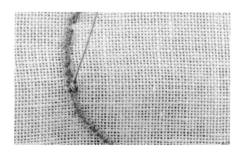

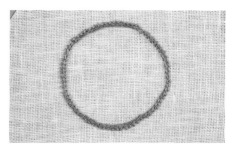

7. Pull the thread to complete the first chain stitch.

8. For subsequent stitches, insert the needle into the previous chain, in the same hole as where the thread emerged. Bring the needle out the same distance along as before. Take the thread under the needle point, then pull the needle through.

9. Once the entire circle of chain stitch is complete, finish the thread by running it under a few stitches on the wrong side of the fabric. The motif border is now complete.

Stitch the Buttonhole Wheels

Half buttonhole wheels can be stitched in a scalloped pattern around the coral stitch and chain stitch motif border to create a decorative outline. Start the thread by running it under a few of the stitches on the wrong side of the fabric. Work the same quantity of stitches for each scallop for a consistent appearance. You can use this technique to stitch full buttonhole wheels as well.

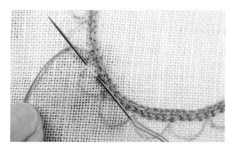

1. Bring the thread out on the outline at the beginning of one of the scallops. Insert the needle in the center of the scallop and bring it out a short way along the line. Take the thread under the needle point.

2. Continue working buttonhole stitch in a radial pattern, inserting the needle in the same hole at the center of the scallop each time.

3. After completing one scallop, start the next by inserting the needle at the next scallop's center. Bring it out on the outline at the beginning of the scallop.

4. Pull the needle through. Insert the needle at the center again. Bring it out a short way along the line and take the thread under the needle point.

5. Continue around the circle in a counterclockwise direction.

6. When the entire circle of buttonhole wheels is complete, finish the thread by running it under a few stitches on the wrong side of the fabric.

Withdraw the Fabric Threads

After sewing the motif border, the next step is to remove some of the threads inside the shape. Adjust the spacing and quantity of threads to be withdrawn according to the filling stitch to be worked.

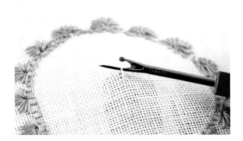

1. On the wrong side of the fabric, insert the seam ripper at the center of the shape to lift up the thread and cut it.

2. A little way from the cut, insert the seam ripper under the thread and ease it out of the fabric. Continue similarly to draw back the cut thread to both sides of the motif.

3. Carefully cut the withdrawn threads at the edge of the shape. Be careful not to cut another thread!

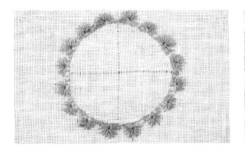

4. When you remove vertical or horizontal withdrawn threads, draw them back from the center to the edges of the shape.

5. Remove further threads as required, according to the individual filling stitch instructions. Carefully withdraw and trim the threads one by one.

AYAKO'S TIPS

What if you cut the wrong thread? Or what if you pull out too much thread? Don't panic. Remove a single thread from the edge of the fabric, then use a blunt-ended needle to weave it back into the fabric at the desired location. This can be a bit tricky, so please be careful when cutting and withdrawing threads.

A Note on Withdrawing Fabric Threads

This book uses a shorthand system to note how to withdraw the fabric threads in preparation for working Schwalm filling stitches. You'll find numbers in parentheses on areas of the templates where Schwalm filling stitches are to be worked. The numbers indicate how many threads to remove and their spacing. For example, (1-3) means to remove one thread, leaving three threads. Repeat this pattern to remove threads from the entire area where Schwalm filling stitches are to be worked. Unless otherwise noted, remove both the vertical and horizontal threads.

a. Wing Stitch

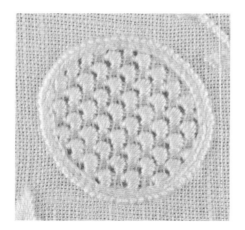
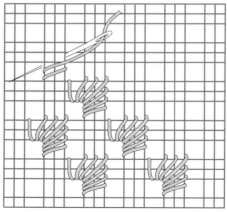

This stitch is named for its resemblance to bird wings. Prepare the fabric by removing one thread and leaving three threads, as represented by 1–3 (refer to page 41).

1. Bring the needle out in a large hole near the edge of the motif. Insert the needle three threads to the right, and bring it out where the thread previously emerged.

2. Pull the stitch tight to draw the fabric threads together.

3. Insert the needle one thread above where it was previously inserted. Bring it out in the same large hole as before.

4. In the same way, continue up the right side of the woven block of three by three threads, then along the top edge, with a stitch between each of the threads.

5. Bring the needle out three threads to the left, and stitch the next wing in the same way.

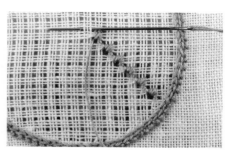

6. Continue stitching diagonally, moving up and left.

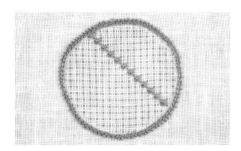

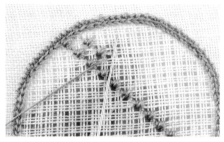

7. One row is complete.

8. Continue sewing the next row back in the opposite direction.

b. Wing Stitch Variation

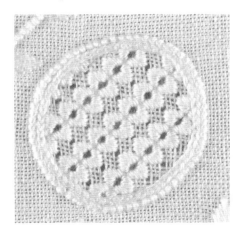

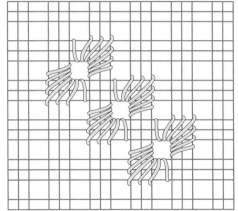

With this variation, the wing stitches are sewn face to face to create a different look.

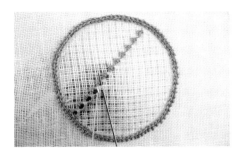

Sew as for wing stitch until step 7 (see pages 42 and above). Work back in the opposite direction, this time with the new row of wings facing the previous row. Work subsequent rows as pairs of facing rows.

c. Rose Stitch

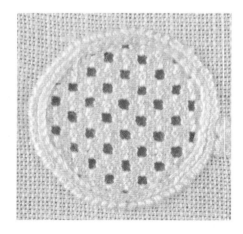
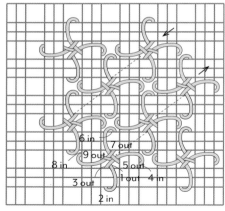

This is a dainty stitch which resembles a wild rose. Insert the needle under groups of threads in four directions to create the stitch. Prepare the fabric by removing one thread and leaving three threads, as represented by 1–3 (refer to page 41).

1. Bring the needle out in a large hole. This will be referred to as the center in subsequent steps. Insert it under the group of three threads below and bring it back to the center.

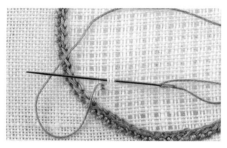

2. Insert the needle under the group of threads to the right and bring it back to the center, taking the thread under the needle point.

3. Insert the needle under the group of threads above and bring it back to the center.

4. Insert the needle under the group to the left and bring it back to the center, taking the thread under the needle point.

5. Pull the thread to finish one motif.

6. Insert the needle in the center of the motif, and bring it out diagonally up and right in the next large hole. This will be the center of the next motif.

7. Repeat steps 1–5 to continue stitching diagonally, moving up and right.

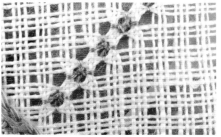

8. Pull the thread as you stitch to draw the threads together. Stitch to the end of the row then turn the work 180 degrees and work back in the other direction. The edges of the next row will share the holes of the edges of this row.

d. Star Rose Stitch

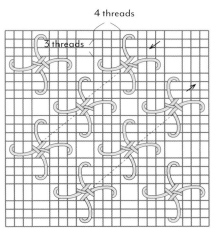

This stitch uses the same basic technique as the rose stitch, but when you stitch under a group, you exclude one thread. The remaining threads form a star pattern. Prepare the fabric by removing one thread and leaving four threads, as represented by 1–4 (refer to page 41).

1. Bring the needle out in a large hole. This will be referred to as the center in subsequent steps. Insert it under the upper three threads of the group of four below and bring it back to the center.

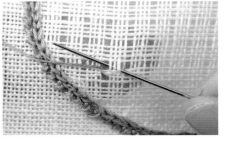

2. Insert the needle under the leftmost three threads of the group to the right of the center.

3. Follow the same process to stitch the upper group then the left group, excluding the outermost thread each time. One stitch is now complete.

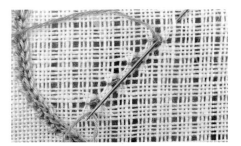

4. To move to the next rose position, insert the needle in the center of the motif, and bring it out diagonally up and right in the next large hole. This will be the center of the next motif. Continue stitching in the same manner.

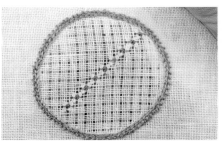

5. Complete the row to the far edge.

6. Turn the work 180 degrees. Stitch the new row in the same way as the first, so that the unstitched thread in each group forms a double cross with the other ones.

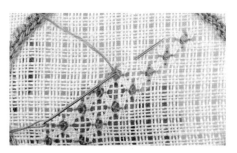

7. Continue stitching.

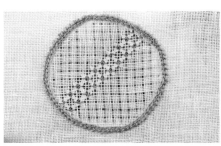

8. The first two rows are complete.

AYAKO'S TIPS ✂

The tension of the thread creates different patterns. Changing the color of the fabric and thread can change the effect greatly.

c. Rose Stitch + e. Wrapped Rosette Stitch

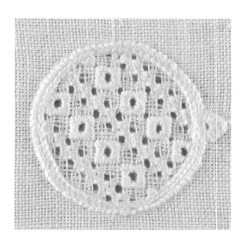

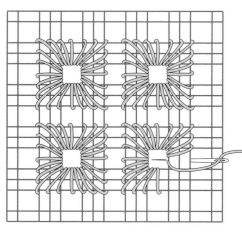

A plump flower stitch is created by wrapping the threads. Here, it is used with rose stitch. Prepare the fabric by removing one thread and leaving three threads, as represented by 1–3 (refer to page 41).

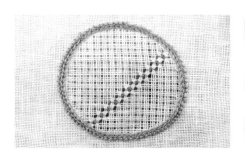

1. Sew one row of rose stitch (see pages 44–45). Counting from the hole shared by the left side of the last rose stitch and top side of the second to last rose stitch, bring the needle out one grid up and left, as shown in step 2. This will be referred to as the center in subsequent steps.

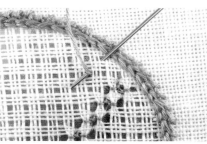

2. Insert the needle in the next large hole diagonally up and right, and then bring the needle back out in the center.

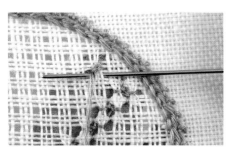

3. Insert the needle one thread below the end of the previous stitch and bring it out again in the center. Continue around the wrapped rosette in a clockwise direction, with one stitch between each of the fabric threads.

4. One motif is complete.

5. Insert the needle under a few stitches on the wrong side of the work to bring the thread closer to the next wrapped rosette position.

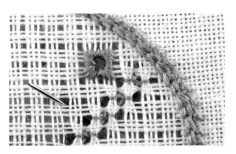

6. Repeat steps 2 to 4 to continue making wrapped rosette motifs.

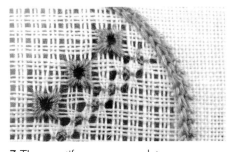

7. Three motifs are now complete.

AYAKO'S TIPS

Here we stitch the rows diagonally, but you can also stitch them horizontally when the pattern is made up of only wrapped rosette motifs.

f. Stair Step Diamond Stitch

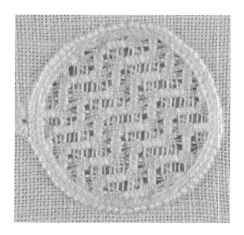 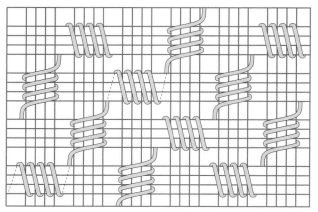

This is a stitch that climbs in steps, block by block. Prepare the fabric by removing one thread and leaving four threads, as represented by 1–4 (refer to page 41).

1. Bring the needle out in a large hole, then insert the needle four threads down and one thread to the right. Bring it out again four threads up.

2. Pull the thread, then insert the needle under the group, one thread to the right. Bring it out again four threads up. Note that the needle is straight and the stitch is slanted.

3. After completing one motif (a total of four stitches), the next one will be worked over the next group of threads diagonally up and right.

4. Stitch the next motif in the same manner, but insert the needle under the group from the right, emerging on the left.

5. The next one will be worked over the next group of threads diagonally up and right. It will be worked in the same orientation as the first motif.

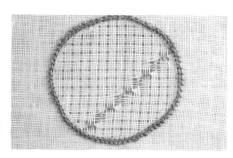

6. Work the row on the diagonal, stepping each group up and right, and alternating the orientation of each one. The first row is complete.

7. Turn the work 180 degrees. Drop down to the second woven square below the last one of the previous row. If it was stitched horizontally, stitch this one vertically, or vice versa.

8. Stitch the row so that horizontal groups and vertical groups alternate.

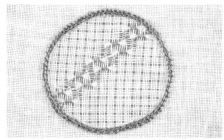

9. The second row is complete.

g. Basic Stitch

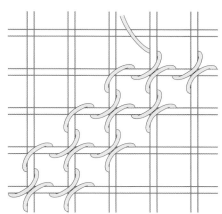

The basic stitch is a pulled thread stitch. It creates a simple ladder shape and is often used in combination with other stitches. With this technique, you'll need to prepare the fabric by removing two threads and leaving two threads, as represented by 2–2 (refer to page 41).

1. Bring the needle out at the edge of the border. From the right, take the needle horizontally under a pair of vertical threads.

2. From above, take the needle vertically under the adjacent pair of horizontal threads.

3. Repeat steps 1 and 2 to continue stitching diagonally up and right.

4. After sewing to the far edge, turn the work 180 degrees, then sew the next row back in the same way.

5. The first two rows of stitching are complete. Continue in the same way.

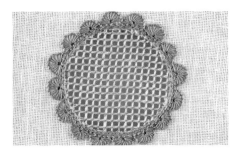

6. Here, the entire circle motif is filled with basic stitch.

g. Basic Stitch + c. Rose Stitch

After completing steps 1–6 on pages 49 and above, add rows of rose stitch on top for an intricate design.

1. Refer to steps 1–8 on pages 44–45 to sew a row of rose stitch on the completed base of basic stitch.

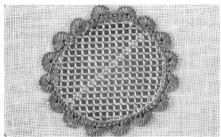

2. One row of rose stitch is complete.

3. Change direction and sew another row of rose stitch across the opposite diagonal.

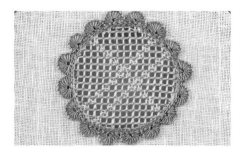

4. Continue sewing rows of rose stitch. A new pattern is created at the intersection of the rose stitch rows.

c. Rose Stitch + h. Wrapping Stitch

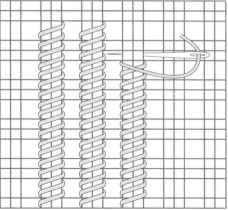

As the name suggests, this stitch groups threads by wrapping them together. It is often used in combination with other stitches, such as the rose stitch shown here. Prepare the fabric by removing one thread and leaving three threads, as represented by 1–3 (refer to page 41).

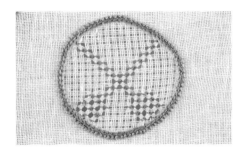

1. Sew rose stitch (see pages 44–45) in a cross shape diagonally across the center, then sew three rose stitches on each side of the ends of the two legs.

2. Next, you'll fill the remaining section with wrapping stitch. The needle is inserted horizontally under the group of three threads.

3. Stitch between each thread. In areas where a cross thread has been removed, work two wrapped stitches. Pull each stitch tight.

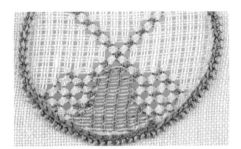

4. Wrapping stitch is complete.

i. Waffle Stitch

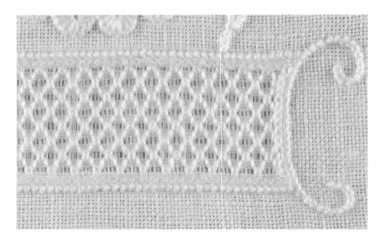

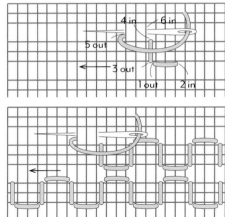

With this stitch, the finished design resembles a waffle weave. Prepare the fabric by removing one horizontal thread and leaving three threads, as represented by 1–3 (refer to page 41).

1. Bring the needle out three threads from the edge in a withdrawn thread line. Insert the needle three threads to the right and bring it out in the same position as before.

2. Tighten the stitch, then insert the needle three threads up. Take the needle under the next three threads to the left.

3. Insert the needle three threads to the right and bring it out in the same position as before. Tighten the stitch, then insert the needle three threads down. Take the needle under the next three threads to the left.

4. Move up and down sewing backstitches, group by group.

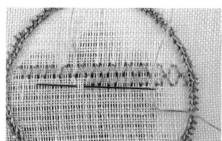

5. Sew to the edge, then turn the work 180 degrees, and stitch the new row as before.

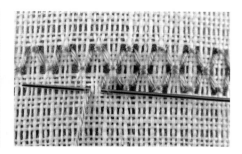

6. As for the first row, move up and down sewing backstitches, group by group.

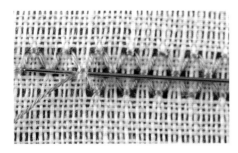

Remember to take the needle under three threads each time.

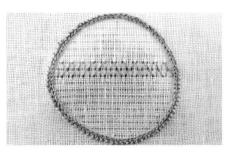

7. Two rows are complete.

Waffle stitch is used to create the nose and feet for the Teddy Bear Pillow on page 106.

Hedebo Embroidery

These are the basics of the technique called "udklipshedebo" or Hedebo needlelace. This style features cutwork with needlelace fillings, and additional motifs worked on the surrounding fabric in surface embroidery.

Stitch the Edging: Hedebo Buttonhole Stitch

This stitch is often worked around the perimeter of a piece to create a base for decorative needlelace, such as buttonhole scallops and pyramids. It is done on a folded fabric edge. Regular buttonhole stitches are usually sewn with the needle pointing away from you, while Hedebo buttonhole stitches are worked with the needle pointing toward you. The initial row of stitching is worked with a sharp-pointed needle. For the second row, use a tapestry or blunt-ended needle.

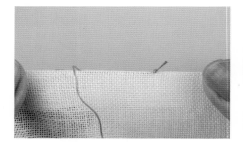

1. Knot the thread and insert the needle into the folded edge of the fabric, 1¼–1½ in (3–4 cm) to the right of the starting point. Bring the needle out at the starting point through the folded edge.

2. Insert the needle from back to front, a little way down from the folded edge.

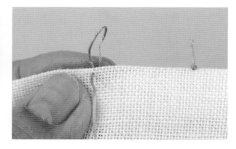

3. Pull the thread through but leave a loop sitting up.

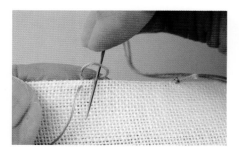

4. Pass the needle through the loop from back to front.

5. Pull the thread upward. One Hedebo buttonhole stitch is complete.

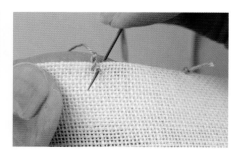

6. Insert the needle from back to front, a little to the right of the previous stitch.

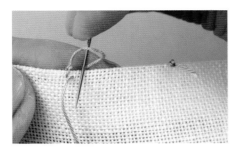

7. Pull the thread through, leaving a loop. Pass the needle through the loop from back to front, then tighten.

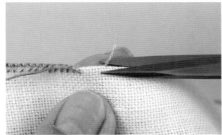

8. After sewing for an inch, cut the knot off. Be careful not to cut the fabric!

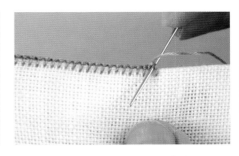

9. After sewing the length required, change to a tapestry needle to work the second row. From the back, insert the needle under the top section between the last two stitches.

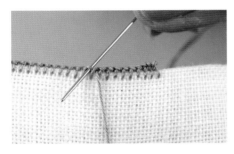

10. Pull the needle through. Continue, passing the needle between each of the stitches in the first row, from back to front.

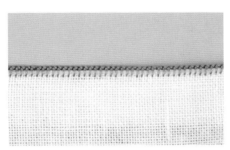

11. The second row is complete. This will serve as a base for needlelace designs.

AYAKO'S TIPS

When you are using an evenweave fabric, count the threads to create regular spacing for the stitches.

j. Buttonhole Scallop

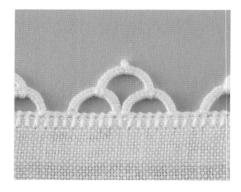

This is a simple but effective method for stitching edges. The buttonhole scallop can also be used to edge open work. It is a versatile stitch as you can layer a few rows or add picots. Use a tapestry or blunt-ended needle for this technique.

First Row

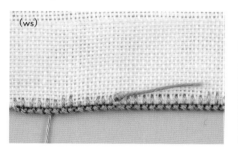

1. Using a base of Hedebo buttonhole stitch (see pages 54–55), insert the needle from the wrong side into the stitched fold, and bring it out on the right side at the edge of the fabric fold.

2. Moving five stitches along, insert the needle into the stitching from the back to front.

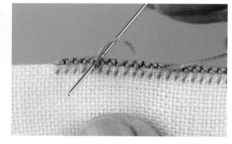

3. Pull the thread length to make an arc, then bring the needle out from the wrong side where you came out the first time.

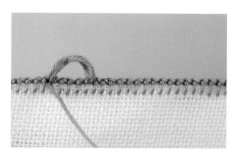

4. Repeat steps 2 and 3 to build up an arc with four stitches, all of the same length. Make the arc a little smaller than the size of the scallop you want to make.

5. Next, you'll work Hedebo buttonhole stitch around the arc. Insert the needle through the arc from back to front.

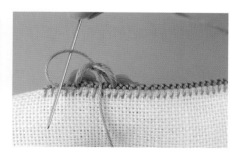

6. Pull the needle through, leaving a small loop. Insert the needle through the loop from back to front.

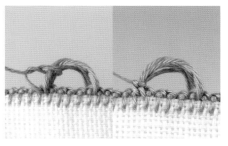

7. Pull the thread toward the left and tighten. One Hedebo buttonhole stitch is complete.

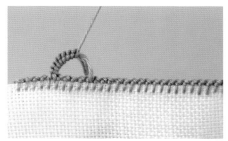

8. Continue to work Hedebo buttonhole stitch around the arc.

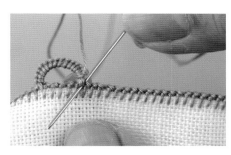

9. Fill the arc with stitches. When you reach the end, insert the needle at the base of the arc from back to front.

10. Work one more Hedebo buttonhole stitch.

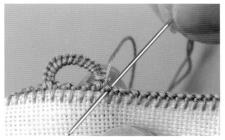

11. One buttonhole scallop is complete. To start the next scallop, insert the needle into the next stitch of the base from back to front.

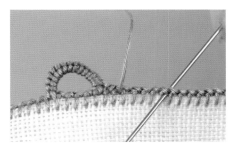

12. Moving five stitches along, insert the needle into the stitching from back to front.

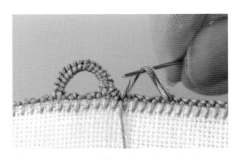

13. Create an arc of four threads and adjust to make it the same size as the inside of the first scallop. This will ensure that the finished buttonhole scallops are equal in size.

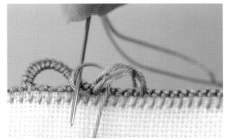

14. Repeat steps 5–7 to work Hedebo buttonhole stitch.

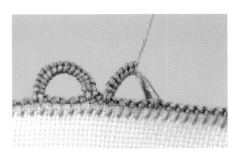

15. Continue working Hedebo buttonhole stitch around the arc, or stop halfway and continue with step 16 to add an additional row.

Second Row

You can layer multiple rows of buttonhole scallops to create unique shapes and patterns.

16. Work the Hedebo buttonhole stitch until you reach the middle of the last arc of the first row (the second arc in this photo). Insert the needle into the center of the previous arc from back to front.

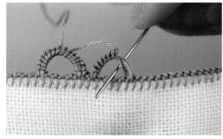

17. Next, insert the needle through the half-worked arc from back to front.

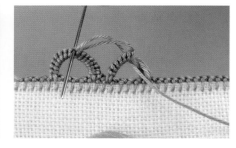

18. Make three stitches in this way to create a new arc, then work Hedebo buttonhole stitch to make a scallop.

AYAKO'S TIPS

You can layer many rows of scallops. Make the desired quantity of scallops in the first row, and after working half of the last scallop, move up to the next row. Don't worry about finishing the other half of the last scallop in the previous row—you'll go back and complete this later as shown in steps 27 and 28 on the next page.

Picots

Knotted picots can be added to scallops for further decoration.

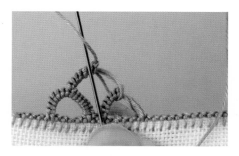

19. Align the needle at the point you want to add the picot.

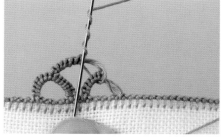

20. Wrap the thread around the needle tip three times in a clockwise direction.

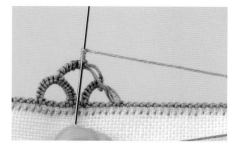

21. Tighten the wraps around the needle so that they sit close to the scallop.

22. Holding the wraps in place, gently pull the needle through.

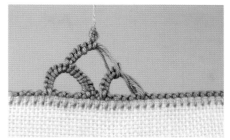

23. Keep pulling until a neat knot sits on the scallop.

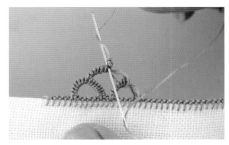

24. Insert the needle at the base of the picot from front to back, then wrap the needle once, clockwise.

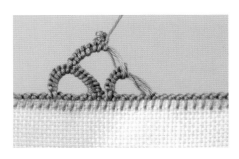

25. Pull the needle through and tighten the stitch.

AYAKO'S TIPS

A picot is similar to a French knot. The size varies depending on how many times you wrap the thread.

26. Continue to work Hedebo buttonhole stitch to finish the arc.

27. Go back to the lower row to continue stitching the remaining half of the last scallop.

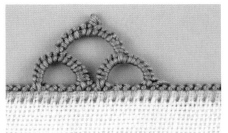

28. Two rows of buttonhole scallops with a picot are now complete.

AYAKO'S TIPS

You can use the same method for any quantity of rows. Move to the next row before finishing the previous row, then complete the remaining half of each scallop in the last row.

k. Pyramids

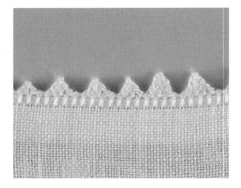

Pyramids are simply triangles composed of Hedebo buttonhole stitches. You can vary the size of the stitches or combine pyramids with buttonhole scallops to create more complex designs. Pyramids are commonly used on the edge of the fabric, but can also be incorporated as part of the open work. Use a tapestry or blunt-ended needle for this technique.

1. Start using a base of Hedebo buttonhole stitch (see page 54). Bring the needle out at the starting point, then insert the needle after the next stitch to the right.

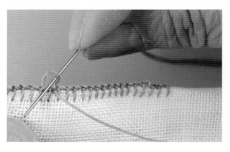

2. Work Hedebo buttonhole stitch onto the base. Note: In the example photos, the thread is left loose to show it clearly, but tighten the thread when you stitch.

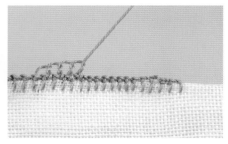

3. Work the desired quantity of Hedebo buttonhole stitches. Four stitches are shown in this example.

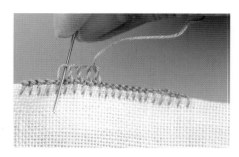

4. After working one row, go back to the first stitch and insert the needle from back to front.

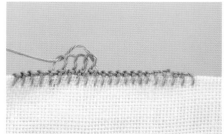

5. Pull the thread so that it sits horizontally. Do not tighten it too much—it should not pull the ends of the row in.

6. Take the needle under the horizontal thread and the stitch next to the first one.

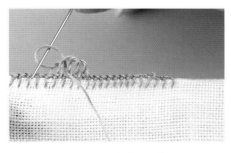

7. Work Hedebo buttonhole stitch to create the second row.

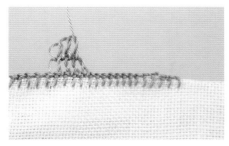

8. The second row should have one less stitch than the previous row. Three stitches are shown in this example.

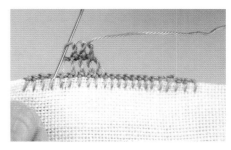

9. Go back to the first stitch of the row and insert the needle from back to front.

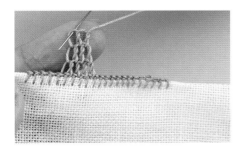

10. Continue working one less Hedebo buttonhole stitch to complete each subsequent row. This will create the triangular shape.

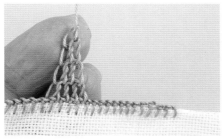

11. To complete the last row, draw the thread upward and make the tip sharp.

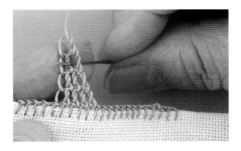

12. Insert the needle through the rightmost stitch of the previous row, from back to front.

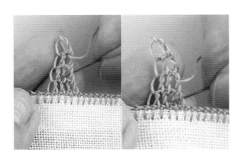

13. Insert the needle through the rightmost stitch one row lower, from back to front. Continue in this manner to stitch down row by row.

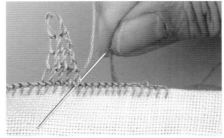

14. At the end, insert the needle at the base of the pyramid.

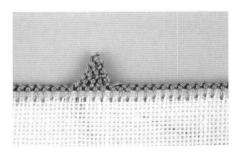

15. When you actually sew, remember to make the stitches tight, as shown here.

Set Up the Open Work

Cut Hedebo has open work, where motifs are worked in holes created by cutting the fabric. The method is different from Schwalm, where you remove the thread within a frame, as this involves cutting fabric to make a hole. First, sew double running stitch, and as you cut the fabric inside, sew Hedebo buttonhole stitch to hem the edges. Both sharp-pointed needles and blunt-ended needles are used for this technique.

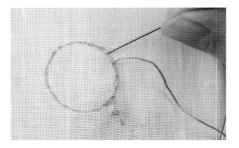

1. Make a knot and insert the sharp-pointed needle from the outside of the design. Sew running stitch along the line.

2. After sewing one circuit, sew a second circuit between the stitches of the first circuit to fill the gaps.

3. Two rounds of running stitch are complete. This is known as double running stitch.

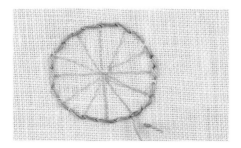

4. Draw a vertical and a horizontal line along the fabric grain to divide the circle into four quarters. Next, draw diagonal lines to divide the circle into 12 sections (each quadrant will have three sections). Make sure one of the lines ends at the last stitch made in step 3.

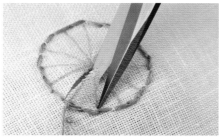

5. Next, you'll use sharp, fine-pointed scissors to cut along the lines. To start, insert the scissors at the center and cut toward the last stitch made in step 3. Be careful not to cut the thread! Use the same process to cut the adjacent line.

6. After cutting one segment along the drawn lines only, fold the flap to the wrong side of the fabric. Press the fold. Insert the needle from the wrong side, bringing it out outside the stitched line.

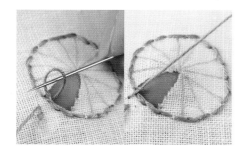

7. Make one Hedebo buttonhole stitch (see page 54).

8. Decide the quantity of stitches per segment (this example uses three), and sew with slightly wider spacing as compared to the base for Hedebo buttonhole stitch.

9. Continue working around the circle, cutting each new segment as you come to it, folding the flap to the wrong side, and stitching. Change to the blunt-ended needle after sewing one circuit. Insert the needle under the first stitch of the first circuit, from back to front.

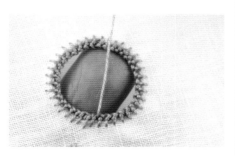

10. Insert the needle under the next stitch to the left, from back to front.

11. Insert the needle under each of the stitches of the first circuit. This stitching travels in the opposite direction to the first circuit (counterclockwise in this example).

12. Return to the starting position. The open work frame is complete.

I. Ladder Stitch

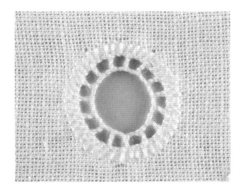

Worked on top of the base shown on page 62 and above, this method creates a ladder-shaped lace filling. Its simplicity and light finish make this stitch a popular choice for both open work and edge stitching. Use a tapestry or blunt-ended needle for this technique.

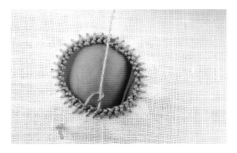

1. Using a base of Hedebo buttonhole stitch (see page 62 and above), insert the needle a few stitches along, from back to front (three stitches away in this example).

2. Pull the thread to create a loop. Insert the needle into the loop from back to front.

3. Pull the thread to complete one stitch. The method is the same as Hedebo buttonhole stitch. The difference is in the spacing.

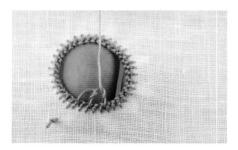

4. Continue to stitch using the same spacing as in step 1.

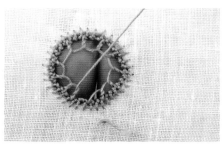

5. Continue working around the circle, using the same spacing, and working the loops all with similar lengths.

6. After completing a circuit, insert the needle into the first loop from back to front.

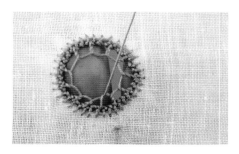

7. Pull the thread. Now the end is joined to the beginning of the circuit.

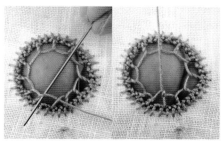

8. Traveling in the opposite direction, insert the needle into the stitch to the left, from back to front.

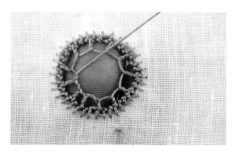

9. Continue, inserting the needle into each of the stitches of the first circuit. This is the same as sewing Hedebo buttonhole stitch.

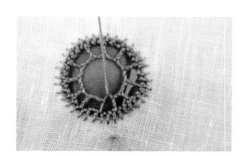

10. Continue around the circle.

11. To complete the circuit, insert the needle into the first stitch of the current row, from back to front.

12. Insert the needle from front to back on the right side of foot of the first stitch.

 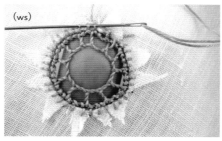 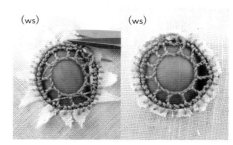

13. The needle is now on the wrong side of the fabric.

14. Insert the needle under a few Hedebo buttonhole stitches to secure the thread.

15. Trim any excess fabric from the flaps that were folded to the wrong side.

Fill the Open Work

Fill open work with motifs composed of various stitches, such as ladder stitch, buttonhole scallops, and pyramids. Work from the edge of the open work toward the center, then connect to the other side. You can add another stitch at the cross section of connected threads. When you sew inside of the open work, trace the design onto separate fabric and baste under the frame, using it as a guide. This will also prevent the fabric from stretching.

Stitch and Connect Motifs

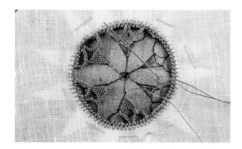  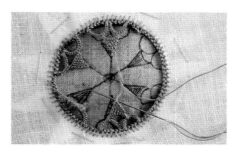

1. Stitch three combination motifs, and then when you've reached the tip of the fourth, insert the needle into the tip of the opposite motif, from back to front.

2. Pull the needle through, and pass it underneath the stitch.

3. Wrap the thread around the stitch three times, then pull the thread to tighten the stitch. Insert the needle at the tip of the unfinished motif, from back to front. This joins the motifs.

4. Stitch down the side of the pyramid to whip each of the end stitches (see page 61).

5. Complete the unfinished buttonhole scallop.

6. Stitch the remaining combination motifs, joining opposite motifs as you work. Instructions for working the center intersection are shown on page 66.

m. Spider Web Stitch

In Hedebo open work, stitches are often worked at the intersection where the individual motifs connect. There are a number of different stitches that can be used for this purpose, but here we'll focus on a simple round stitch called the spider web. Note: In the example photos, the thread is left loose to show it clearly, but tighten the thread when you stitch so the spider web stitch looks like the example photo shown at left.

Needle will be here after completion of step 6 on page 65

1. Go back one spoke and take the needle under the thread held by the finger, then under the spoke ahead working in a clockwise direction. Drawing the thread through will create a little bump around the spoke. Next, weave over, under, over, under the remaining four spokes, working in a clockwise direction.

2. Rotate the work one segment clockwise. Bring the needle out at the center of the spokes. Working in a counterclockwise direction, pass the thread over the first spoke, then under the next one.

3. Because the number of spokes is even, you cannot scoop alternately. Take the needle over the next two spokes, then under the final one.

4. Continue weaving around the circle in a counterclockwise direction. Alter the location of the two spokes you pass over on each circuit.

5. Continue weaving in this manner.

6. When the spider web is large enough, take the needle under the closest stitch in the previous circuit.

7. Take the needle under the nearest spoke to return to the tip of the unfinished motif.

8. Finish stitching the final motif (refer to page 59).

9. The spider web stitch and the Hedebo open work motif are complete.

Open Work for Other Shapes

In Hedebo open work, variation comes from both the general shape of the design and the stitching method used to fill the inside. Complicated designs can be wonderful, but even simple stitches can be used to create interesting patterns. Try combining different stitches or altering the positioning for a unique look. The balance of the cut areas and remaining area of fabric is also important. You can achieve this balance by adding substantial embroidery motifs to the non-cut area of the fabric.

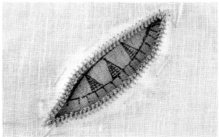

Open work for cut Hedebo is not always worked in circles. In this book, you'll see designs for raindrops, crescents, rectangles, and leaf shapes.

When you sew the filling, draw the pattern on separate fabric, then position it underneath to use as a guide as shown in the picture.

Drawn Thread Work

This is a type of open work, sometimes called "drawn work." With this technique, threads are withdrawn from the fabric. Stitches are worked on the remaining fabric threads to create beautiful patterns. It is a basic method of whitework embroidery and is often used as a border on various embroidered goods. The embroidery can be quite simple, or if you remove more threads and sew more complicated stitches in the drawn thread areas, it can be even more delicately beautiful. In this book, simple drawn thread work is used so that it is not too difficult. Use tapestry needles to sew as you count the fabric threads.

Withdraw the Fabric Threads

In the area where you wish to withdraw the thread, cut the thread at the center. Withdraw the thread along the length of the drawn thread area.

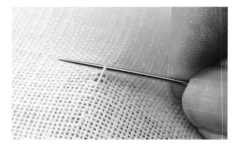

1. Lift up the thread at the center of the area from which it needs to be removed.

2. With fine-pointed scissors, carefully cut the thread.

3. Move along the thread to be withdrawn and insert the needle under it. Gently lever the thread up and out of the fabric.

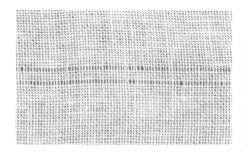

4. Withdraw the thread on both sides of the cut made in step 2. This example shows two threads that have been withdrawn with four threads remaining in between. Do not trim the withdrawn threads.

5. To finish the thread ends: Take the withdrawn threads to the wrong side. Thread a tapestry needle with one of the withdrawn threads. Insert the needle in the row above or below, and following the weave of the fabric, weave the thread back into the fabric.

6. Weave for about ⅜ in (1 cm). Trim the thread end. Repeat for the other thread ends.

n. Four-Sided Stitch

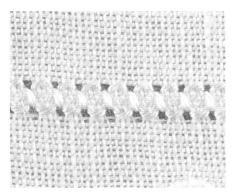

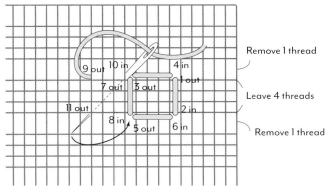

Remove 1 thread

Leave 4 threads

Remove 1 thread

As you stitch, small squares are formed. This is usually worked on both sides of drawn thread borders, but can also be worked by itself as a simple border without withdrawing fabric threads, as shown on page 86. For drawn thread work, prepare the fabric by removing horizontal threads as shown in the diagram above. You will always make your stitches into the holes made by the withdrawn threads.

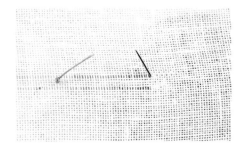

1. Make a knot and insert the needle about 1¼ in (3 cm) to the left of the starting point. Bring the needle out at the starting point.

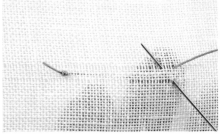

2. Insert the needle four threads down, then bring it out four threads diagonally up and left.

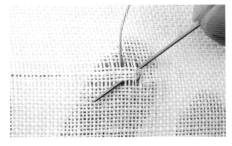

3. Insert the needle four threads to the right (back at the starting point), then bring it out four threads diagonally down and left.

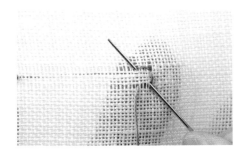

4. Insert the needle four threads to the right, then bring it out four threads diagonally up and left, at the same position as in step 2.

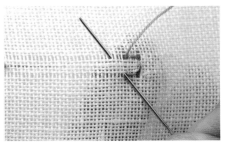

5. Repeat steps 2–4, and pull the stitch tight each time.

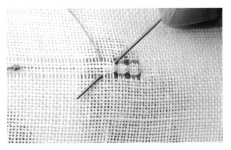

6. Continue making small squares in the same way. This technique will create a cross pattern on the wrong side, as shown in the step 8 photo.

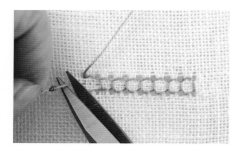

7. When you reach the knot from step 1, pull slightly and cut the excess thread.

8. The thread end is already secured on the wrong side, so you don't need to finish it.

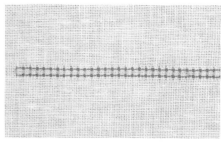

9. Continue to stitch in the same way. Finish the thread end by taking it under a few stitches on the wrong side of the fabric.

o. Zigzags with Four-Sided Stitch

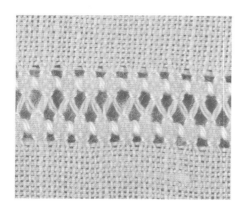

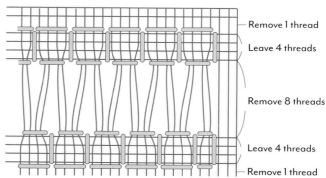

Remove 1 thread
Leave 4 threads
Remove 8 threads
Leave 4 threads
Remove 1 thread

With this technique, threads are removed and manipulated to create a zigzag pattern between two rows of four-sided stitch. Prepare the fabric by removing horizontal threads as shown in the diagram above.

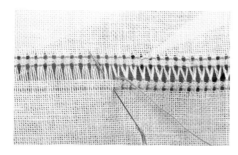

1. Work four-sided stitch along the top of the drawn thread area. Continue working four-sided stitch along the bottom. Note that the first group of the bottom row will span only two threads horizontally (refer to the step 3 image).

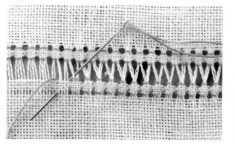

2. This photo shows how the groups of four threads at the top will be divided and regrouped with two each from adjacent groups for the bottom row.

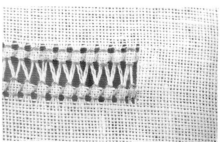

3. The first group on the bottom row will span only two threads horizontally.

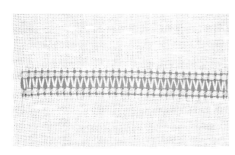

4. Continue to stitch. The last group of the bottom row will also span only two threads horizontally.

p. Double Wrap Stitch

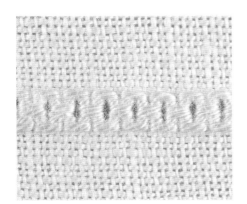

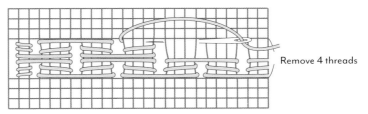

Remove 4 threads

This is a simple stitch made by wrapping groups of threads together. You'll wrap halfway along each thread group, first from the bottom, and then from the top. Prepare the fabric by removing horizontal threads as shown in the diagram above.

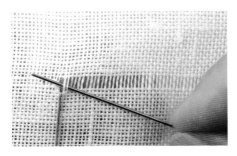

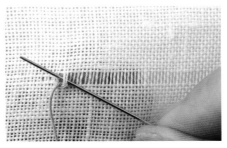

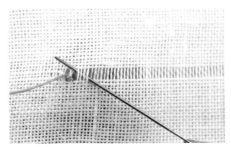

1. Bring the needle out at the bottom left. From the right, insert the needle under the first two threads.

2. Above the previous stitch, insert the needle under the same two threads again.

3. From the right, insert the needle under the next four threads to the right. When the stitch is tightened, the thread should come out below the stitch.

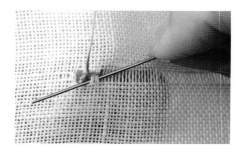

4. From the right, insert the needle under the same four threads, just below the previous stitch.

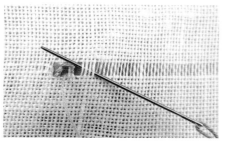

5. From the right, insert the needle under the next four threads to the right. When the stitch is tightened, the thread should come out above the stitch.

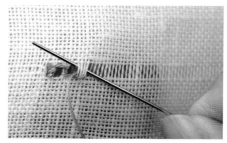

6. Above the previous stitch, insert the needle under the same four threads again.

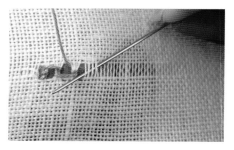

7. From the right, insert the needle under the next four threads. When the stitch is tightened, the thread should come out below the stitch.

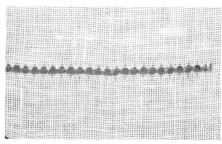

8. Continue wrapping groups of four threads twice, moving up and down. The stitching should cover only half the height of the drawn thread area.

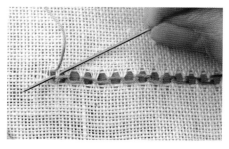

9. Next you'll fill in the remaining drawn thread area with symmetrical stitching. From the right, insert the needle under the first two threads.

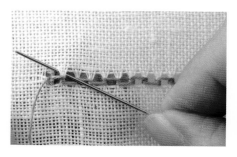

10. Wrap the same threads once more, then, insert the needle under the next four threads, from the right.

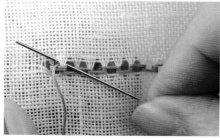

11. Moving up, wrap the same four threads again.

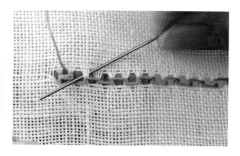

12. From the right, insert the needle under the next four threads.

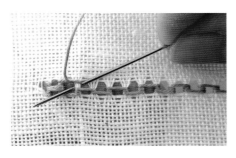

13. Moving down, wrap the same four threads again.

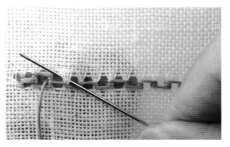

14. Moving to the right, insert the needle under the next four threads, from the right.

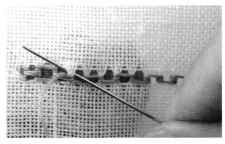

15. Moving up, wrap the same four threads again.

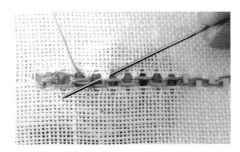

16. Continue in the same way to wrap each group of four threads twice, in a mirror image to the first line of stitching.

How to Prepare a Corner for Drawn Thread Work

If a design requires you to remove many vertical and horizontal threads as is common with drawn thread work corners, do not remove them all at once as the fabric may destabilize. Instead, remove them one by one and then stitch over that section as soon as possible.

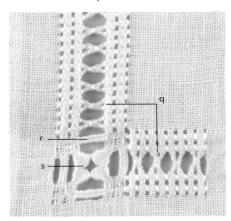

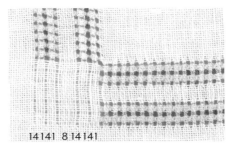

1. Remove the threads one by one in the order of 1–4–1–4–1–8–1–4–1–4–1, and sew two sets of two lines of four-sided stitch.

2. Remove eight threads (both vertically and horizontally) between the two lines of four-sided stitch.

q. Single Peahole Stitch

This stitch reminds me of peas in peapods. It is worked from the wrong side of the fabric.

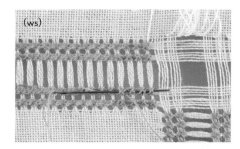

1. Anchor the thread under the back of the stitching.

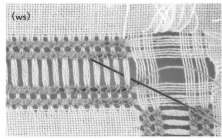

2. From the right, take the needle under the first four threads at the right end.

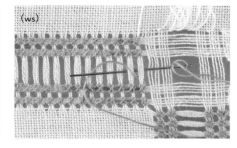

3. Moving up, take the needle under the same four threads and the next four. Make sure to take the thread up over and then down behind the needle point.

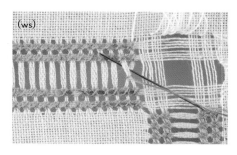

4. Pull to tighten the stitch halfway up the drawn thread area. This will manipulate the threads into an X-shape. Insert the needle above the stitch, under the left group of threads.

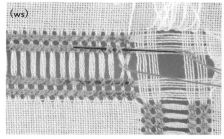

5. Take the needle under the back of the second and third four-sided stitch squares from the right in the row at the upper edge.

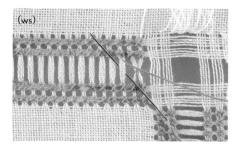

6. From the right, take the needle under the next group of four threads.

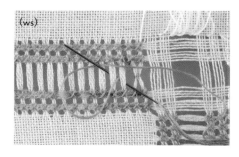

7. Moving down, take the needle under the same four threads and the next four. Make sure to take the thread down over and then up behind the needle point.

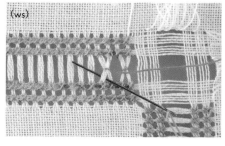

8. Pull to tighten the stitch halfway down the drawn thread area. Insert needle below the stitch, under the left group of threads.

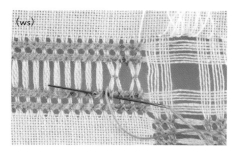

9. Take the needle under the back of the fourth and fifth four-sided stitch squares from the right in the row at the lower edge.

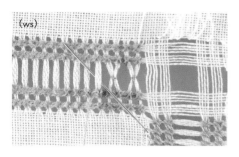

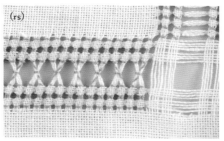

10. Continue in the same manner, moving up and down tying the twinned groups of threads together.

11. This is the view from the right side of the fabric.

r. Needleweaving

This is a simple stitch worked back and forth between groups of threads.

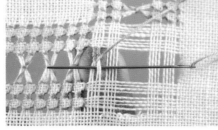

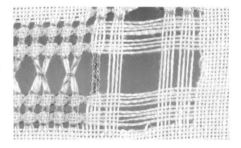

1. Anchor the thread in the back of nearby stitching. Bring the needle out in the middle of the group of four threads adjacent to the peahole stitch. Insert the needle from the left, under the two left threads, coming up again in the middle.

2. Insert the needle from the right, under the two right threads, coming up again in the middle.

3. Continue along the threads, weaving them together in a figure eight shape to create a narrow bar.

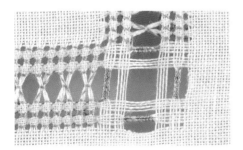

4. Work the remaining three bars in the same way.

s. Corner Darning Stitch

Stitch the thread in a figure eight shape to create a decorative corner.

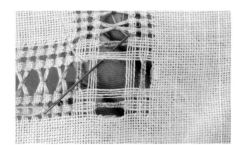

1. Bring the needle out from the outside of the top left corner. Then from below, insert the needle under the group of four horizontal threads at the top.

2. From the right, insert the needle under the group of four vertical threads on the left.

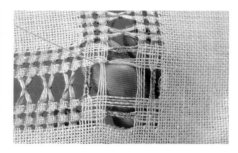

3. Insert the needle under the group of four horizontal threads at the top, then under the group of four vertical threads on the left.

4. Continue weaving back and forth between the left vertical threads and the top horizontal threads. Be careful not to pull the thread too hard, making longer stitches as you progress.

5. When half the bar is woven, take the needle under the top four horizontal threads to move to the top right corner.

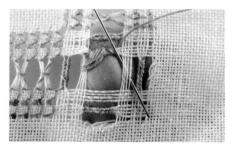

6. From the left, take the needle under the group of four vertical threads on the right.

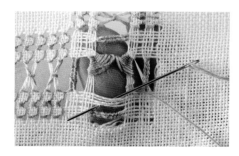

7. Weave back and forth. When half the right bar is full, move on to the bottom right corner by taking the needle under the bottom four horizontal threads.

8. When all the corners are complete, bring the thread to the wrong side. Insert through a corner inside the stitching and finish it under the back of nearby stitching.

Broderie Anglaise

Broderie Anglaise is a kind of whitework which reached England around the beginning of the 19th century. The technique features eyelets, which are holes where the edges are bound with stitching. It is often used for children's clothing, blouses, and underwear. Use a sharp-pointed needle.

t. Eyelet

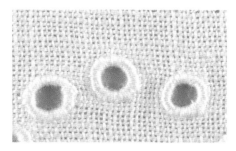

Use this technique to make eyelets in a variety of sizes.

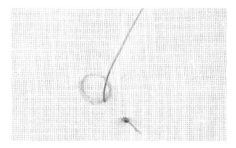

1. Draw a circle of the required size. Make a knot at the thread end, insert the needle a short distance away from the circle, and bring it out at the edge of the circle.

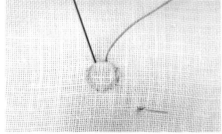

2. Sew running stitch along the circle.

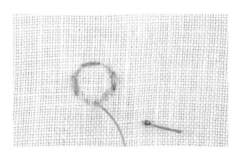

3. One circuit is complete.

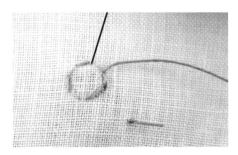

4. Stitch between the stitches of the first circuit to create double running stitch.

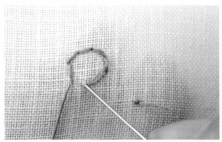

5. When the two circuits are complete, the thread returns to the starting point.

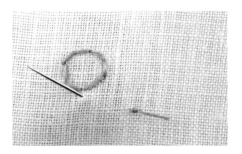

6. Bring the needle out a little way outside of the running stitch. This distance represents the width of the eyelet stitching.

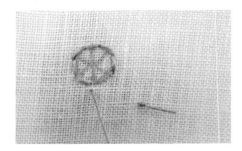

7. Draw lines inside the circle to divide it into six segments. One of the lines should end near where the thread comes out.

8. Next, you'll use sharp, fine-pointed scissors to cut along the lines. To start, insert the scissors at the center and cut along the line where the thread comes out. Be careful not to cut the thread! Use the same process to cut the adjacent line.

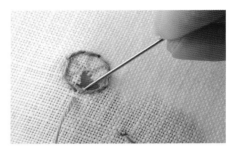

9. Fold the flap to the wrong side. Insert the needle in the center.

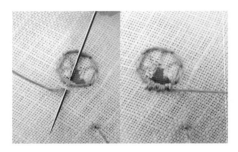

10. Bring the needle out right next to the previous stitch. Continue overcast stitching around the circle, positioning the stitches as close together as possible and making them equal in length.

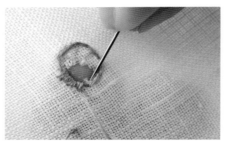

11. Cut the next segment, fold the flap to the wrong side, and sew in the same manner.

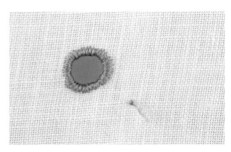

12. One round is complete.

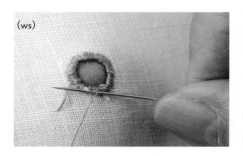

13. On the wrong side of the fabric, run the needle under the back of a few stitches to finish the thread.

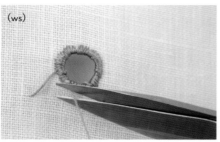

14. Trim the excess thread.

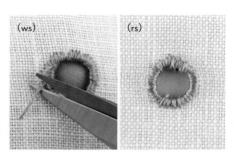

15. Cut the knot made in step 1 to complete the eyelet.

About Coton a Broder Thread

Introduced on page 38, coton a broder is a loosely twisted thread commonly used for whitework embroidery. Whitework embroidery originally used linen or silk thread, but in recent times, coton a broder has become more popular. Its unique shine and twist means it matches well with linen or cotton fabric. Also, the soft thread blends well with the fiber of the fabric, and creates a very clean finished look. However, if you repeatedly make mistakes and use it again, the thread will deteriorate and lose its shine. Expert stitchers can create very shiny finished items. If the thread of a finished item is shiny, it is proof you have mastered that embroidery!

Eyelet Variation

Teardrop shapes are commonly used in addition to circular eyelets.

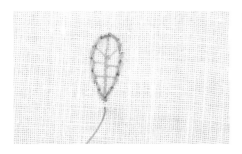

1. Sew double running stitch along the shape, then draw the lines to cut the inside. Draw the lines so that you can fold the fabric back as easily as possible.

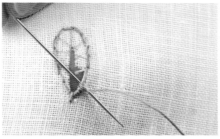

2. Cut each section one by one and overcast stitch the folded edge.

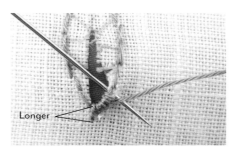

Longer

3. Make longer stitches for sharply-pointed areas.

4. The teardrop eyelet is complete. If there is excess fabric on the wrong side, trim as described on page 65.

AYAKO'S TIPS

If you sew very fine running stitches underneath, the fabric tends to wrinkle. When making a small eyelet hole, instead of using a base of running stitch, sew a chain stitch or lazy daisy stitch around the circle or teardrop guide to make a base, and then make a hole using an awl.

Counted Thread Work

Counted thread work refers to styles of embroidery where the stitches are positioned by counting the threads of the fabric. Cross-stitch is one style of counted embroidery. Counted embroidery can be seen in early examples of Hedebo embroidery. Straight stitch and satin stitch are commonly used in this technique.

u. Double Cable Stitch

This stitch is worked with paired diagonal rows of stitching. Use a blunt-ended needle.

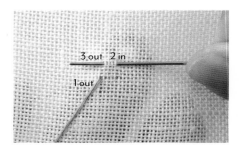

1. Bring the needle out in the bottom left of a four by four thread square, and insert it four threads up and right. Bring it out four threads to the left.

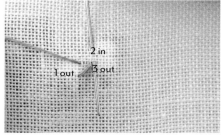

2. Insert the needle four threads up and right. Bring it out again four threads down.

3. Repeat steps 1 and 2 to continue. Two parallel diagonal lines are created as you sew.

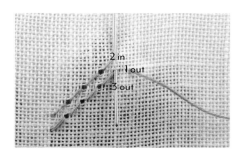

4. After sewing the tip of the corner, bring the needle out four threads down and right. Insert the needle back in the tip (four threads up and left), and bring it out four threads down.

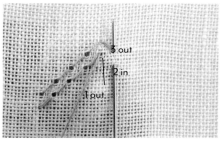

5. To start sewing the other side, insert the needle four threads down and right. Bring it out four threads up.

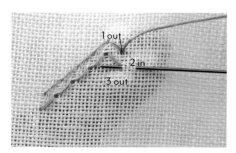

6. Insert the needle four threads down and right. Bring it out four threads left. Repeat steps 5 and 6 to continue.

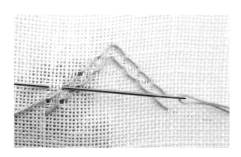

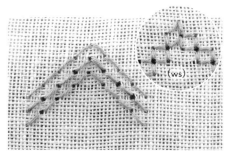

7. Start a new row of stitching, coming out in the same hole as for the upper line of the first row. Insert the needle four threads up and right. Bring it out four threads left. Note that the lower edge of the second row shares holes with the upper edge of the first row, meaning the middle line of stitching has paired stitches.

8. At the corner tip, bring the needle out four threads down and right, and insert it four threads up and left. Bring the needle out four threads down.

9. The double cable stitch is complete. Except in the corner, the wrong side shows stepped stitching.

Double cable stitch is used for the Embroidery Tool Case on page 146.

Hvidsøm Embroidery

This is one of seven styles of Hedebo embroidery. Hvidsøm means "white stitching." It was primarily worked from the 1830s to the 1850s. The drawn thread work areas are surrounded with chain stitch. It was in this Hedebo style that the technique of removing fabric threads within shapes first appeared, and designs such as flowers and plants became popular. Compared to Schwalm embroidery that influenced Hedebo later, this style is simple and strong.

Withdraw the Woven Threads

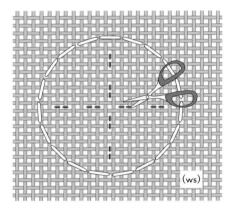

1. Sew double running stitch around the motif (see page 62), then cut the threads as marked.

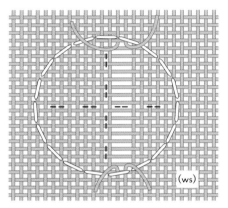

2. Remove the woven thread little by little (refer to page 41), and leave the withdrawn thread hanging on the wrong side. Do not trim the ends yet.

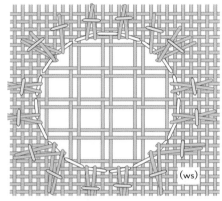

3. Baste to secure the hanging thread ends a little way out from the running stitch.

Work Filling Stitches

x. Cross-Stitch

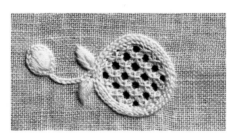

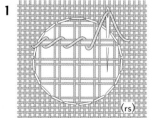

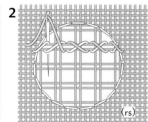

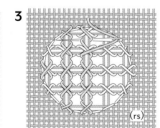

Work cross-stitches vertically and horizontally. Sew over the intersecting threads in one direction, and then back to create crosses.

v. Cross-Stitch + Whipped Stitch

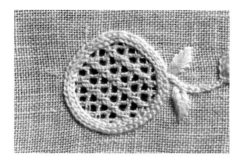

1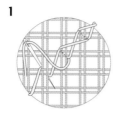

2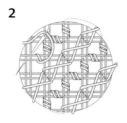

Working diagonally, sew crosses in a line. Then work a diagonal line where each group of threads is whipped twice.

w. Cross-Stitch + Whipped Stitch + Needleweaving

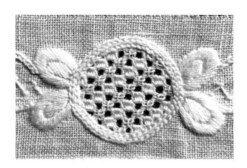

Between lines of cross-stitch, make two lines of whipped stitch Vs, and then sew needleweaving stitch (see page 75) over them.

Chain Stitch Around the Edge

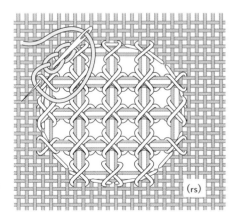

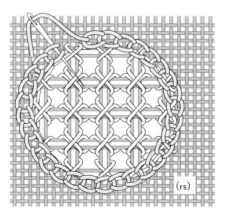

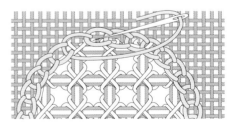

1. After working the desired filling stitches, sew chain stitch around the edge of the motif.

2. The chain stitch will hide the line of double running stitch and hold the withdrawn thread ends on the wrong side of the fabric.

3. Join the final stitch as shown in the diagram. Sometimes, another round of chain stitch is added outside the first. On the wrong side, remove the basting and trim the thread ends near the chain stitch.

Pulled Thread Work

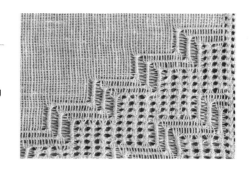

In pulled thread work, the stitches are pulled tight to create holes in the fabric, which form patterns. Use open weave fabric which has easily moved threads, and sew using a blunt-ended needle. The appearance changes depending on how tight you pull each stitch, so tighten the stitches with a consistent tension throughout.

A. Wrapped Stitch

Blocks of satin stitch are pulled tight. Each subsequent row has the pulled and unpulled sections offset to create patterns.

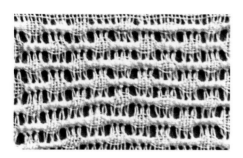

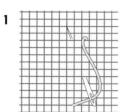

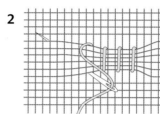

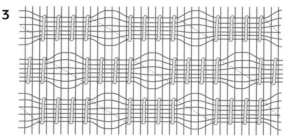

B. Chessboard Filling Stitch

Work seven tightly pulled satin stitches spanning three threads. Take the thread through the wrong side of the stitches to move from the first column to the second column, then make seven more stitches. Step down diagonally after each pair is stitched. Work horizontal stitches one way, then fill the spaces between with vertical stitches.

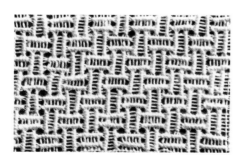

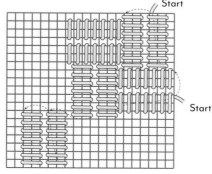

C. Checker Filling Stitch

Sew parallel rows of cross-stitch diagonally, then sew more rows of cross-stitch perpendicular to the first rows, across the top of them.

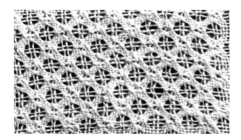
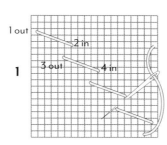
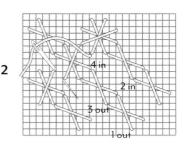

D. Step Stitch

Sew five tightly pulled satin stitches spanning four threads. Alternate between vertically and horizontally stitched blocks.

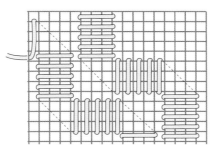

E. Wave Stitch

Bring the needle out at 1, then insert at 2 (four threads down and two right). Go under four threads to the left, coming out at 3. Insert at 1, where the thread first emerged. Go under four threads to the left. Repeat the sequence, pulling all stitches tight as you go to create a diamond pattern.

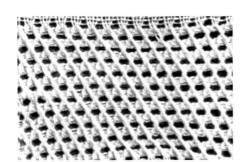
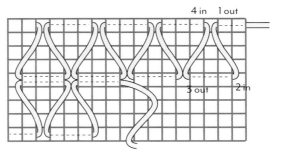

F. Greek Cross Filling Stitch

Sew in the numerical order noted below to stitch in a cross shape. Continue to sew the next cross diagonally down and right, with one thread in between the two crosses.

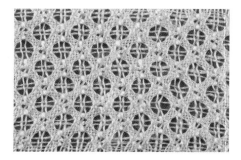
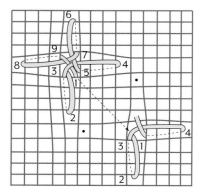

G. Wrapped Stitch + Four-Sided Stitch

Sew a combination of wrapped stitch and four-sided stitch to create an interesting pattern featuring varying horizontal bands.

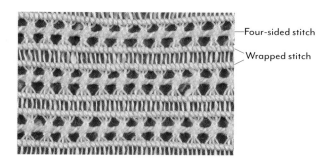

Four-sided stitch

Wrapped stitch

Wrapped Stitch

Four-Sided Stitch

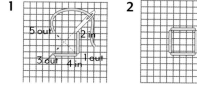
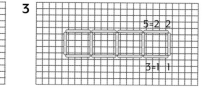

Bring out and insert the needle in the numerical order noted above. Repeat with position 3 becoming the new position 1 for the next square (as noted by 3=1). Sew as many squares as are required.

H. Cable Stitch

Bring out and insert the needle in the numerical order noted below. Work one row diagonally, and then the second row so that it shares holes with the first.

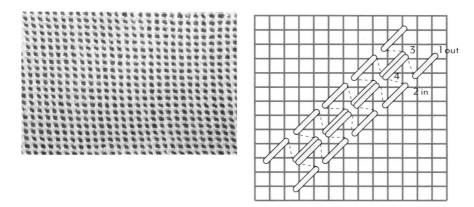

I. Ringed Backstitch

Start from the left side of the hexagon, then move to the right. Come out at the odd numbers and insert the needle at the even numbers. This technique creates a turtle-shaped pattern.

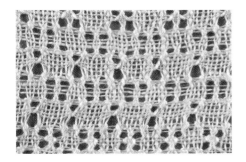
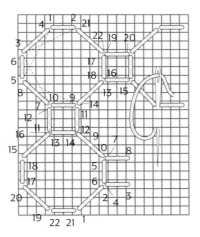

J. Step Stitch + Four-Sided Stitch

This pattern is created from a combination of step stitch (D) and four-sided stitch (G).

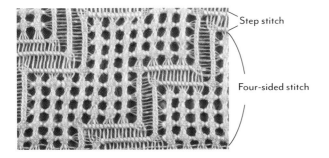

Step stitch

Four-sided stitch

Whitework Sampler I

Shown on page 4

MATERIALS

> Linen fabric: 38 count in white
  − 18 x 23 in (45.5 x 58 cm)
> Thread: DMC coton a broder in
white (B5200)
  − #16: 1 skein
  − #20: 4 skeins
  − #25: 2 skeins
  − #30: 1 skein

FINISHED SIZE

12¼ x 17¼ in (31 x 44 cm)

FULL-SIZE TEMPLATE

Pattern Sheet A

SAMPLER OVERVIEW DIAGRAM

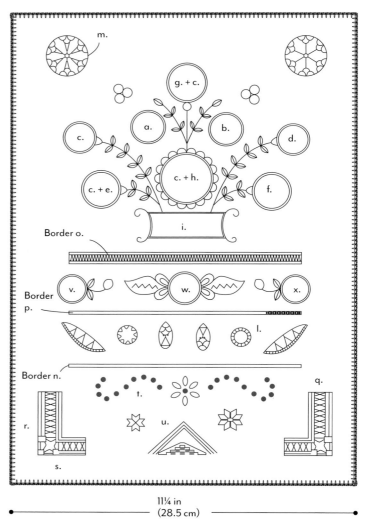

16¼ in
(41 cm)

11¼ in
(28.5 cm)

INSTRUCTIONS

1. Overlock/zigzag stitch the fabric edges so that they do not fray.

2. Use the template on Pattern Sheet A to trace the design onto the center of the fabric.

3. Embroider as noted on the template and in the diagrams below and on pages 90–91.

4. Fold and press the edges over ⅜ in (1 cm) to the wrong side. Sew Hedebo buttonhole stitch on the folded edge, then sew any other edge embroidery as desired. Use the project photo on page 4 for reference, as well as the diagrams on page 91.

Hedebo buttonhole
stitch #20 (see page 54)

(rs)

⅜ in (1 cm)

(ws)

⅜ in
(1 cm)

EMBROIDERY DIAGRAMS

Note: All of the borders are 7¾ in (19.5 cm) wide.

Border o.

Zigzags with four-sided stitch #25 (see page 70)

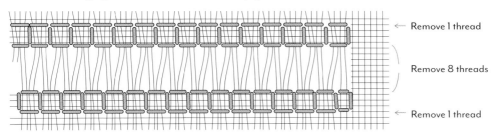

← Remove 1 thread

Remove 8 threads

← Remove 1 thread

Border p.

Double wrap stitch #16 (see page 71)

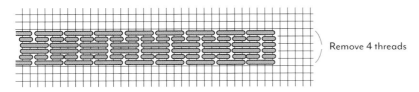

Remove 4 threads

Border n.

Four-sided stitch #25 (see page 69)

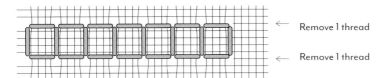

← Remove 1 thread

← Remove 1 thread

Motif u.

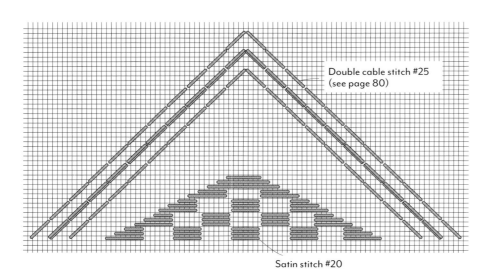

Double cable stitch #25
(see page 80)

Satin stitch #20

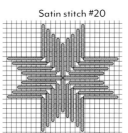

Satin stitch #20

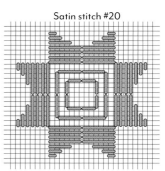

Satin stitch #20

Motifs q. + r. + s.

Use #25 thread for all stitches in this motif.

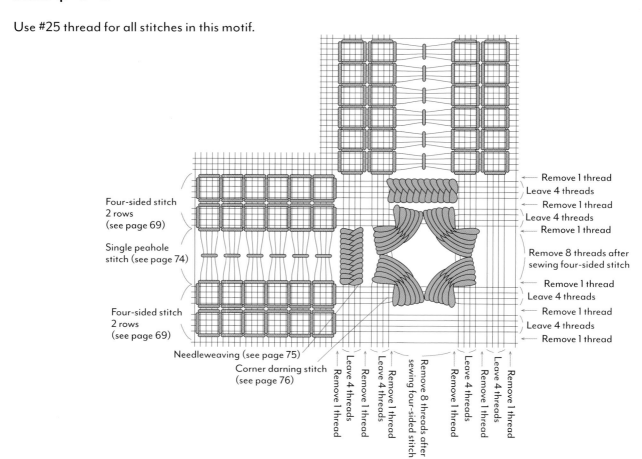

Four-sided stitch
2 rows
(see page 69)

Single peahole
stitch (see page 74)

Four-sided stitch
2 rows
(see page 69)

Needleweaving (see page 75)

Corner darning stitch
(see page 76)

Remove 1 thread
Leave 4 threads
Remove 1 thread
Leave 4 threads
Remove 1 thread

Remove 8 threads after
sewing four-sided stitch

Remove 1 thread
Leave 4 threads
Remove 1 thread
Leave 4 threads
Remove 1 thread

Leave 4 threads
Remove 1 thread
Leave 4 threads
Remove 1 thread
Remove 8 threads after sewing four-sided stitch
Remove 1 thread
Leave 4 threads
Remove 1 thread
Leave 4 threads
Remove 1 thread

Edge Motifs j. + k.

Use #20 thread for all edge embroidery.
See page 56 for buttonhole scallop.
See page 60 for pyramids.
See page 63 for ladder stitch.

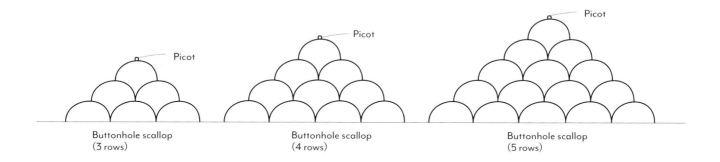

Picot — Picot — Picot

Buttonhole scallop
(3 rows)

Buttonhole scallop
(4 rows)

Buttonhole scallop
(5 rows)

Buttonhole scallops — Picot — Picot

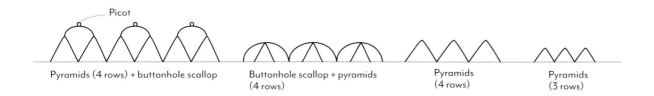

Picot

Pyramids (4 rows) + buttonhole scallop

Buttonhole scallop + pyramids
(4 rows)

Pyramids
(4 rows)

Pyramids
(3 rows)

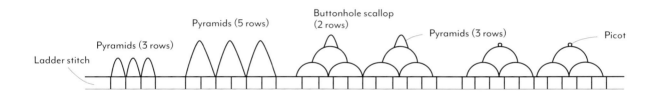

Pyramids (3 rows)

Pyramids (5 rows)

Buttonhole scallop
(2 rows)

Pyramids (3 rows)

Picot

Ladder stitch

Quatrefoil Doily

Shown on page 6

MATERIALS

> Linen fabric: 30 count in white
  – 16 x 16 in (40.5 x 40.5 cm)
> Thread: DMC coton a broder in
white (B5200)
  – #20: 2 skeins
  – #25: 1 skein

FINISHED SIZE

9 x 9 in (23 x 23 cm)

FULL-SIZE TEMPLATE

Pattern Sheet B

INSTRUCTIONS

1. Use the template on Pattern Sheet B and the Stitch Guide on page 93 to trace the cutting lines and embroidery design onto the center of the fabric. Embroider as noted, except the edging.

2. Trim into shape along the cutting lines (which include seam allowance).

3. Fold and press the edges over ⅜ in (1 cm) to the wrong side, clipping the curves where necessary. Sew Hedebo buttonhole stitch on the folded edge.

4. Complete the needlelace edging, as noted on page 93.

9 in (23 cm)

STITCH GUIDE

Use this to trace the embroidery design onto the fabric and to stitch. Use the template on Pattern Sheet B to mark the cutting lines and trim into shape.

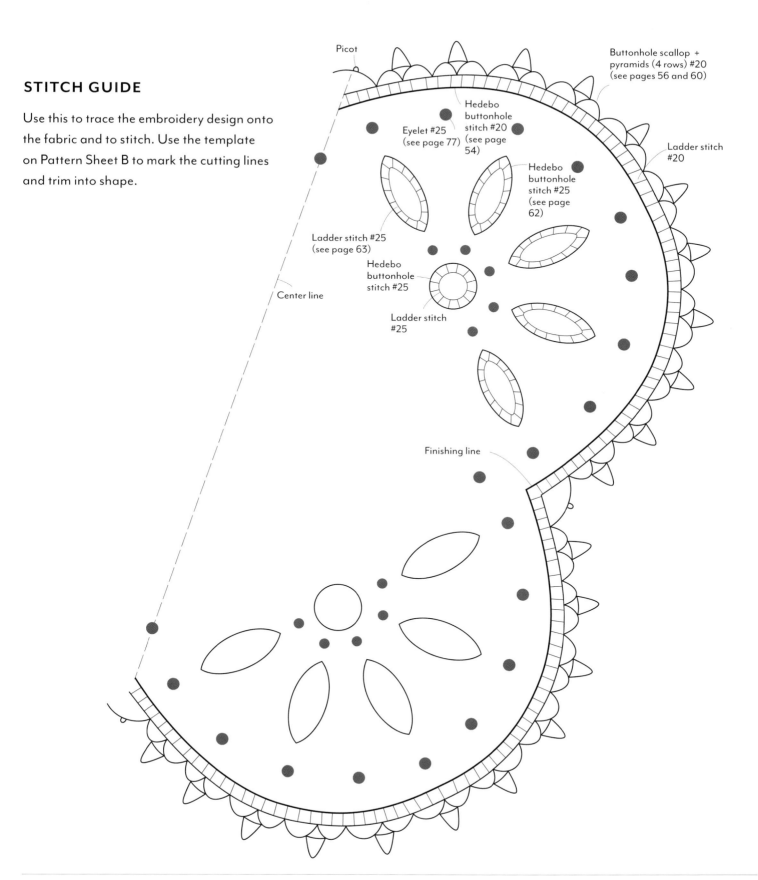

Picot

Buttonhole scallop + pyramids (4 rows) #20 (see pages 56 and 60)

Eyelet #25 (see page 77)

Hedebo buttonhole stitch #20 (see page 54)

Hedebo buttonhole stitch #25 (see page 62)

Ladder stitch #20

Ladder stitch #25 (see page 63)

Hedebo buttonhole stitch #25

Ladder stitch #25

Center line

Finishing line

Edgework Dish Covers

Shown on page 7

MATERIALS (FOR ONE)

> Linen fabric: Finely woven fabric in white
  – 19¾ x 11¾ in (50 x 30 cm)
> Thread: DMC coton a broder in off-white (BLANC) or white (B5200)*
  – #20: 2 skeins

FINISHED SIZE

8 in (22 cm) in diameter excluding needlelace

FULL-SIZE TEMPLATES

Pattern Sheet A

*BLANC was used for the top dish cover sample on page 7, while B5200 was used for the center and bottom dish covers.

INSTRUCTIONS

1. Use the templates on Pattern Sheet A to cut the following pieces out of fabric. Make sure to cut out along the dotted seam allowances lines.

Piece	Quantity
Front	1
Back A	1
Back B	1
Back C	1

2. On the front, fold and press the edge over ⅜ in (1 cm) to the wrong side. Sew Hedebo buttonhole stitch on the folded edge. Next, stitch the desired needlelace edging as shown below.

Top Cover

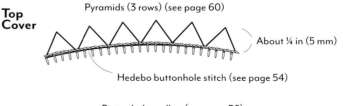

Pyramids (3 rows) (see page 60)

About ¼ in (5 mm)

Hedebo buttonhole stitch (see page 54)

Center Cover

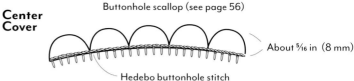

Buttonhole scallop (see page 56)

About 5/16 in (8 mm)

Hedebo buttonhole stitch

Bottom Cover

Pyramids (4 rows) + buttonhole scallop

Picot

About ⅜ in (1 cm)

Hedebo buttonhole stitch

3. On the back pieces, fold and press all the straight edges over ¾ in (2 cm) to the wrong side. Topstitch ½ in (1.3 cm) from the fold to secure the hem in place. Next, fold and press all the curved edges over ⅜ in (1 cm) to the wrong side.

4. With wrong sides together, align backs A and B with the front. Make sure that B slightly overlaps A. Neatly hand stitch the curved edges of A and B to the wrong side of the front, stitching through the Hedebo buttonhole stitches made in step 2.

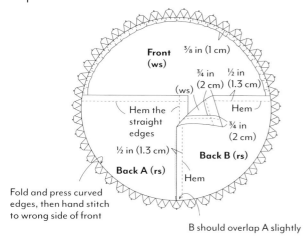

Front (ws)
⅜ in (1 cm)
¾ in (2 cm)
½ in (1.3 cm)
(ws)
Hem the straight edges
Hem
¾ in (2 cm)
½ in (1.3 cm)
Back B (rs)
Back A (rs)
Hem

Fold and press curved edges, then hand stitch to wrong side of front

B should overlap A slightly

5. With wrong sides together, align back C with the front. It should slightly overlap A and B. Use the same process to hand stitch the curved edge of C to the wrong side of the front.

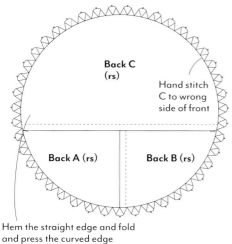

Back C (rs)
Hand stitch C to wrong side of front
Back A (rs)
Back B (rs)

Hem the straight edge and fold and press the curved edge

FINISHED DIAGRAMS

Top Cover

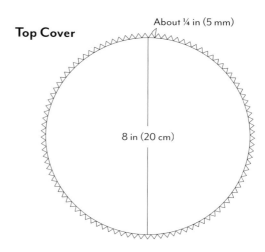

About ¼ in (5 mm)
8 in (20 cm)

Center Cover

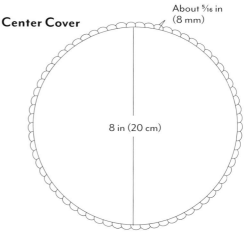

About ⁵⁄₁₆ in (8 mm)
8 in (20 cm)

Bottom Cover

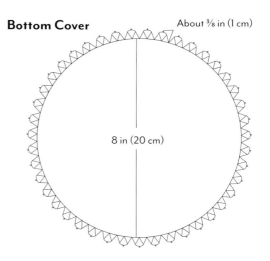

About ⅜ in (1 cm)
8 in (20 cm)

Teapot Cozy

Shown on page 8

MATERIALS

> Linen fabric for embroidery: Finely woven fabric in white
  - 33½ x 17¾ in (85 x 45 cm)
> Thread: DMC coton a broder in white (B5200)
  - #20: 4 skeins
  - #25: 1 skein
> Cozy fabric: Cotton or linen fabric in gray
  - 16½ x 26¾ in (42 x 67 cm)
> Lining fabric: Cotton or linen fabric in white
  - 16½ x 26¾ in (42 x 67 cm)
> Fusible fleece: 26 x 9½ in (66 x 24 cm)

FINISHED SIZE

13 in (33 cm) wide x 9½ in (24 cm) tall x 2 in (5 cm) deep

FULL-SIZE TEMPLATES

Pattern Sheet B

INSTRUCTIONS

1. Use the template on Pattern Sheet B to trace the cutting lines and embroidery design onto the white linen fabric for the front. Leave a bit of space, then trace just the cutting lines of the template for the back.

2. Embroider the front as noted on the template, except the edging. Trim both the front and back into shape along the cutting lines (which include seam allowance).

3. On both the front and back, fold and press the scalloped edges over ⅜ in (1 cm) to the wrong side, clipping the curves where necessary. Sew Hedebo buttonhole stitch on the folded edge, then complete the needlelace edging as noted on the template. Set these pieces aside.

Front

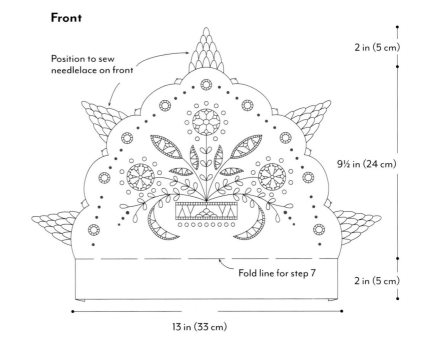

Position to sew needlelace on front

2 in (5 cm)

9½ in (24 cm)

Fold line for step 7

2 in (5 cm)

13 in (33 cm)

Back

Note: The position of the needlelace alternates with the front

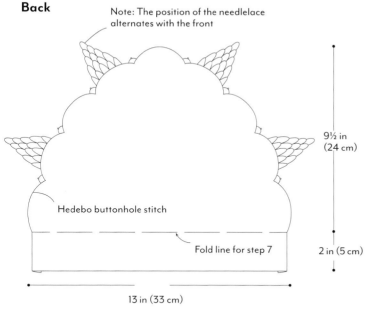

9½ in (24 cm)

2 in (5 cm)

Hedebo buttonhole stitch

Fold line for step 7

13 in (33 cm)

5. With right sides together, sew the gusset to the curved edges of the two outside pieces. Adhere fusible fleece to the wrong side of the linings, then use the same process to sew the gusset lining to the two lining pieces.

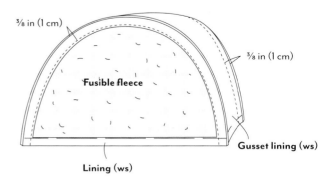

⅜ in (1 cm)

⅜ in (1 cm)

Fusible fleece

Gusset lining (ws)

Lining (ws)

*The outside will be assembled the same way, but will not have fusible fleece.

4. Use the template on Pattern Sheet B and dimensions noted below to cut the following pieces out of fabric. Both the template and dimensions include ⅜ in (1 cm) seam allowance.

6. Insert the outside into the lining with wrong sides together. Fold and press the bottom seam allowances in. Topstitch around the bottom. Turn right side out.

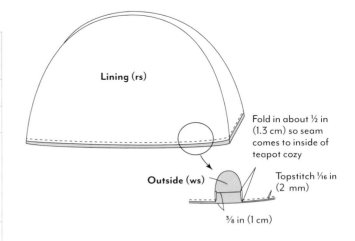

Lining (rs)

Fold in about ½ in (1.3 cm) so seam comes to inside of teapot cozy

Outside (ws)

Topstitch ¹⁄₁₆ in (2 mm)

⅜ in (1 cm)

Piece	Quantity	Fabric	Template or Dimensions
Outside	2	Cozy	Outside/Lining
Lining	2	Lining	Outside/Lining
Fusible fleece	2	Fusible fleece	Outside/Lining (cut along finishing lines so pieces do not have seam allowance)
Gusset	1	Cozy	2¾ x 26⅜ in (7 x 67 cm)
Gusset lining	1	Lining	2¾ x 26⅜ in (7 x 67 cm)

7. Using the pieces set aside in step 3, hand stitch to connect the front needlelace edging to the corresponding scallops on the back and vice versa. Fold and press the bottom raw edge of the front and back over ⅜ in (1 cm) to the wrong side. Next, fold and press the edge over another 1½ in (4 cm) using the fold line marked on the template. Slip the assembled front and back over the teapot cozy from step 6. Hand stitch the folded edge of the front and back to the lining on the inside of the teapot cozy.

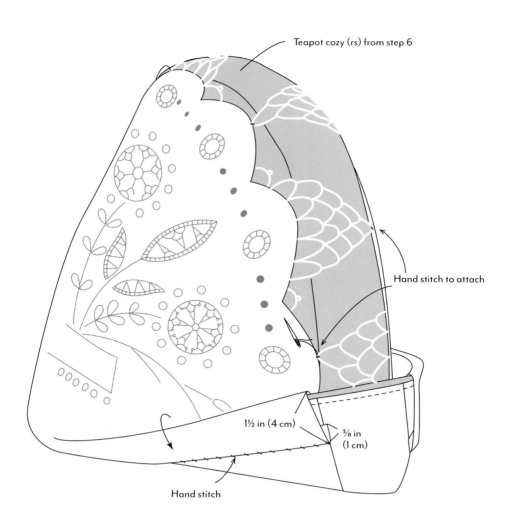

Teapot cozy (rs) from step 6

Hand stitch to attach

1½ in (4 cm)

⅜ in (1 cm)

Hand stitch

Petite Placemats

Shown on page 10

Shown on page 10

MATERIALS

For A

> Linen fabric: 30 count in white
  – 15½ x 15½ in (39 x 39 cm)
> Thread: DMC coton a broder in white
  (B5200)
  – #20: 1 skein
  – #25: 2 skeins

For B

> Linen fabric: 30 count in white
  – 16 x 16 in (40 x 40 cm)
> Thread: DMC coton a broder in white
  (B5200)
  – #25: 1 skein

FINISHED SIZE

A: 8¾ in (22 cm) in diameter
B: 9 x 9 in (23 x 23 cm)

FULL-SIZE TEMPLATES

Pattern Sheet B

INSTRUCTIONS

1. Use the template on Pattern Sheet B and Stitch Guide on page 100 or 101 to trace the cutting lines and embroidery design onto the center of the fabric. Embroider as noted, except the edging.

2. Trim into shape along the cutting lines (which include seam allowance).

3. Fold and press the edges over ⅜ in (1 cm) to the wrong side, clipping the curves where necessary. Sew Hedebo buttonhole stitch on the folded edge.

4. Complete the needlelace edging, as noted in the Stitch Guide.

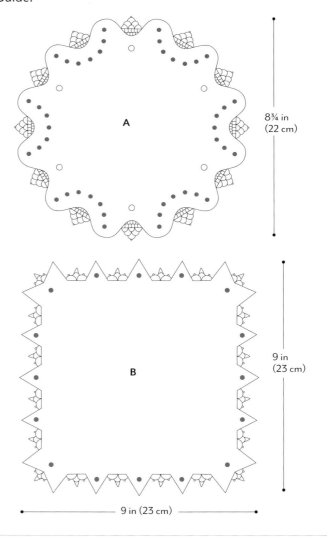

STITCH GUIDES

Use these to trace the embroidery design onto the fabric and to stitch. Use the templates on Pattern Sheet B to mark the cutting lines and trim into shape.

A

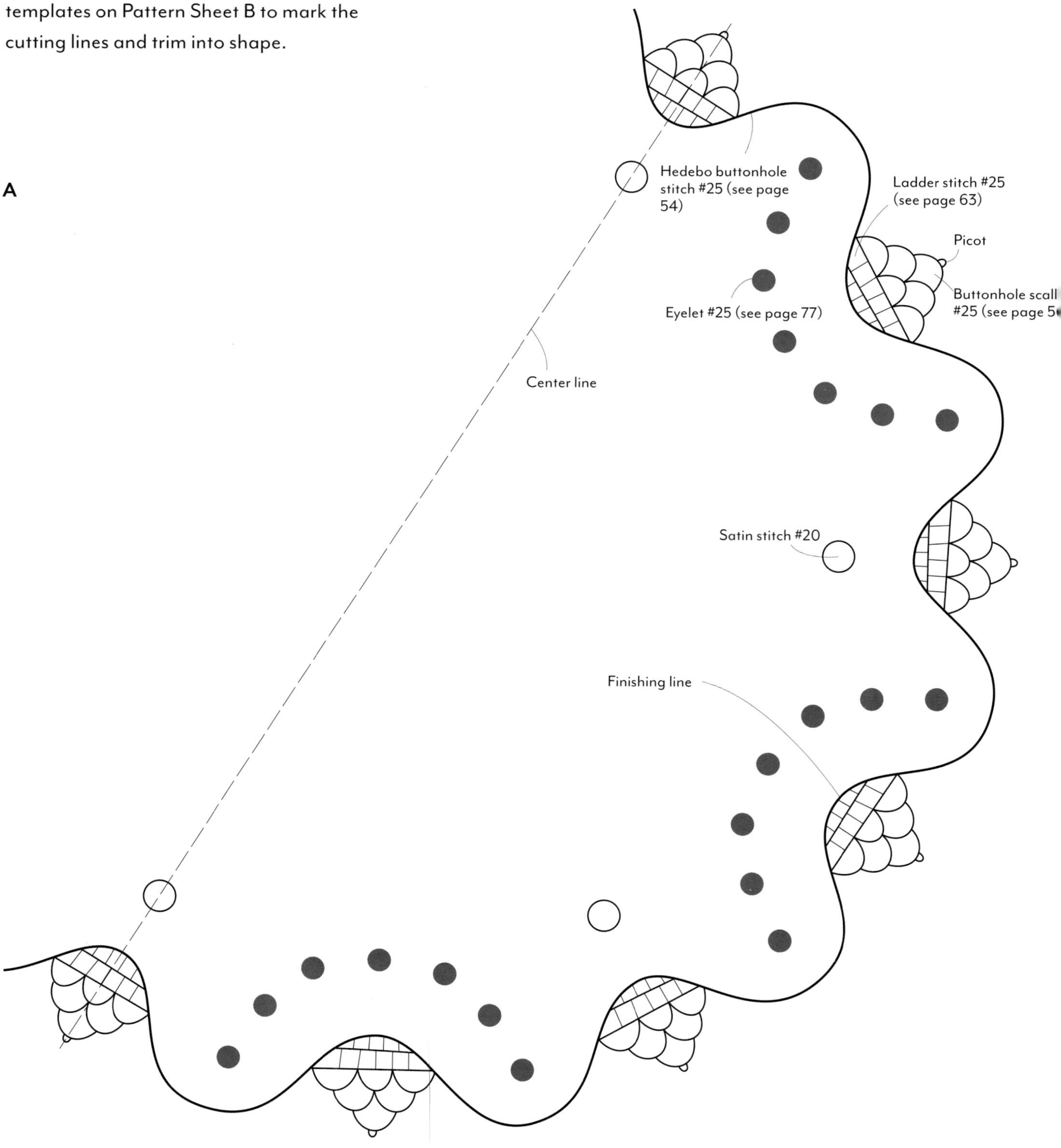

Hedebo buttonhole stitch #25 (see page 54)

Ladder stitch #25 (see page 63)

Picot

Buttonhole scall #25 (see page 5▮

Eyelet #25 (see page 77)

Center line

Satin stitch #20

Finishing line

B

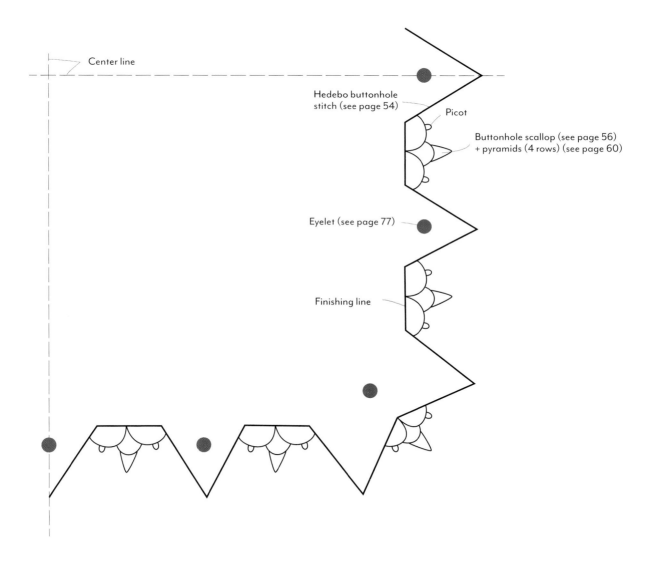

Center line

Hedebo buttonhole
stitch (see page 54)

Picot

Buttonhole scallop (see page 56)
+ pyramids (4 rows) (see page 60)

Eyelet (see page 77)

Finishing line

Floral Cushion

Shown on page 14

MATERIALS

> Linen fabric: 32 count in white
  - 39 x 22 in (99 x 56 cm)
> Thread: DMC coton a broder in white (B5200)
  - #16: 2 skeins
  - #20: 1 skein
  - #25: 1 skein

> 18 in (45.5 cm) square pillow form

FINISHED SIZE

16¼ x 16¼ in (41 x 41 cm)

INSTRUCTIONS

1. Cut a 22 in (56 cm) square of fabric for the front and a 17 in (43 cm) square of fabric for the back.

2. Use the template on page 103 to trace the design onto the center of the front fabric, then embroider as noted. When the embroidery is complete, trim the fabric into a 17 in (43 cm) square.

3. Sew the front and back with right sides together, leaving a 9½ in (24 cm) opening in one side.

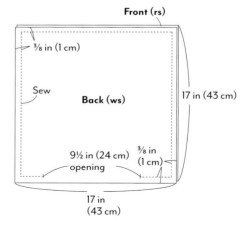

Front (rs)

⅜ in (1 cm)

Sew

Back (ws)

9½ in (24 cm) opening

⅜ in (1 cm)

17 in (43 cm)

17 in (43 cm)

4. Turn right side out through the opening. Insert the pillow form. Fold the opening seam allowances in, and then neatly hand stitch closed.

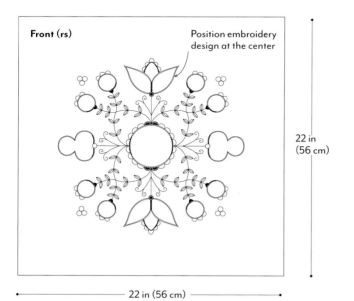

Front (rs)

Position embroidery design at the center

22 in (56 cm)

22 in (56 cm)

FULL-SIZE TEMPLATE

– This design is symmetrical at the center lines. You will need to turn 90 degrees and trace again a total of three times for the full pattern.

– The numbers in parentheses indicate how many threads to remove and their spacing (1–3 means to remove one thread, leaving three threads).

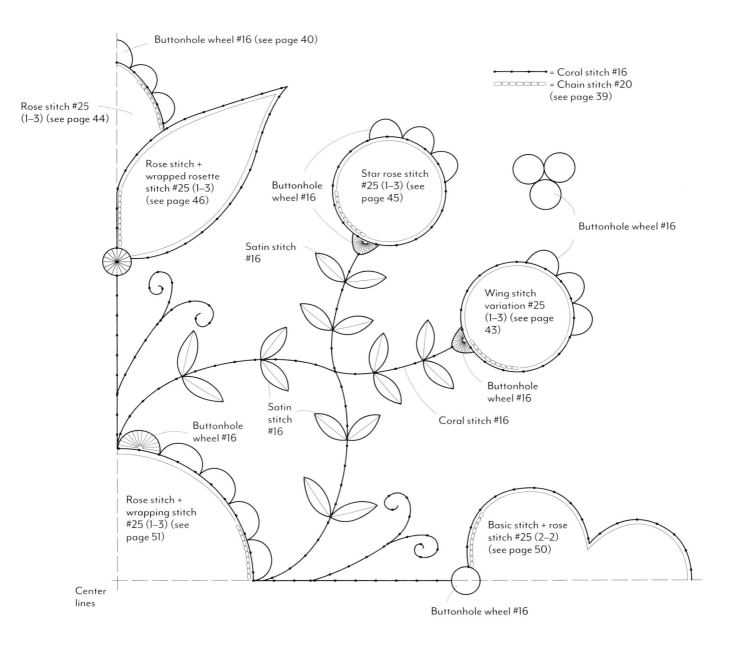

Buttonhole wheel #16 (see page 40)

Rose stitch #25 (1–3) (see page 44)

Rose stitch + wrapped rosette stitch #25 (1–3) (see page 46)

Buttonhole wheel #16

Star rose stitch #25 (1–3) (see page 45)

Satin stitch #16

● = Coral stitch #16
○○○○ = Chain stitch #20 (see page 39)

Buttonhole wheel #16

Wing stitch variation #25 (1–3) (see page 43)

Buttonhole wheel #16

Coral stitch #16

Satin stitch #16

Buttonhole wheel #16

Rose stitch + wrapping stitch #25 (1–3) (see page 51)

Basic stitch + rose stitch #25 (2–2) (see page 50)

Center lines

Buttonhole wheel #16

Snowflake Cushion

Shown on page 15

MATERIALS

> Linen fabric: 25 count in white
  – 40¼ x 22¾ in (102 x 58 cm)
> Thread: Pearl cotton in white (B5200)
  – #8: 1 skein
  – #12: 1 skein

> 18 in (45.5 cm) square pillow form

FINISHED SIZE

16½ x 16½ in (42 x 42 cm)

INSTRUCTIONS

1. Cut a 22¾ in (58 cm) square of fabric for the front and a 17¼ in (44 cm) square of fabric for the back.

2. Starting from the center, work the embroidery as noted in the Stitch Diagram on page 105. Repeat the pattern from the center outward, until there are 21 diamond motifs along the center. When the embroidery is complete, trim the fabric into a 17¼ in (44 cm) square.

3. Sew the front and back with right sides together, leaving a 9½ in (24 cm) opening in one side.

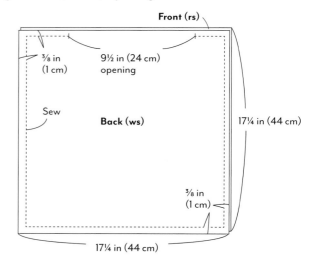

4. Turn right side out through the opening. Insert the pillow form. Fold the opening seam allowances in, and then neatly hand stitch closed.

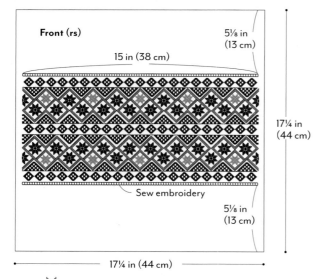

STITCH DIAGRAM

– Count the fabric threads from the center.

– Use #8 unless otherwise noted.

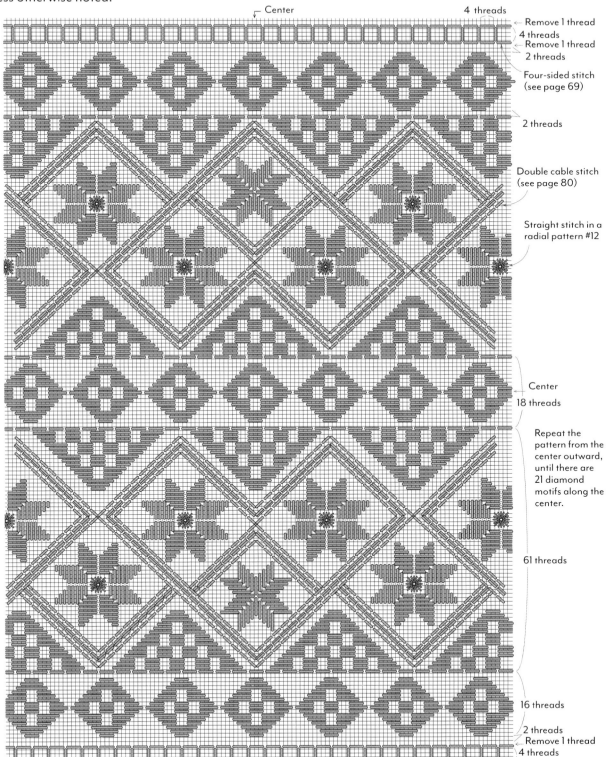

Center

4 threads

← Remove 1 thread

4 threads

← Remove 1 thread

2 threads

Four-sided stitch (see page 69)

2 threads

Double cable stitch (see page 80)

Straight stitch in a radial pattern #12

Center

18 threads

Repeat the pattern from the center outward, until there are 21 diamond motifs along the center.

61 threads

Note: The pillow pictured on page 15 has been rotated 90 degrees.

16 threads

2 threads

← Remove 1 thread

4 threads

← Remove 1 thread

Teddy Bear Pillow

Shown on page 16

MATERIALS

> Linen fabric: 32 count in white
  – 34 x 17 in (86 x 43 cm)
> Thread: DMC coton a broder in white (B5200)
  – #16: 1 skein
  – #20: 3 skeins
  – #25: 1 skein

> 18 in (45.5 cm) square pillow form

FINISHED SIZE

16¼ x 16¼ in (41 x 41 cm)

INSTRUCTIONS

1. Cut two 17 in (43 cm) squares of fabric. These will be the front and back.

2. Use the template on page 107 to trace the design onto the center of the front fabric, then embroider the bear's outlines. Remove the threads within the stitched outlines as noted, then sew the filling stitches. Finally, complete the drawn work border as noted below.

Corner darning stitch (see page 76)

Two lines of four-sided stitch + single peahole stitch (82 motifs) (see pages 69 and 74) *Also refer to page 90

Front (rs)

9¾ in (25 cm)

9¾ in (25 cm)

17 in (43 cm)

Position embroidery design at the center

17 in (43 cm)

3. Sew the front and back with right sides together, leaving a 9½ in (24 cm) opening in one side.

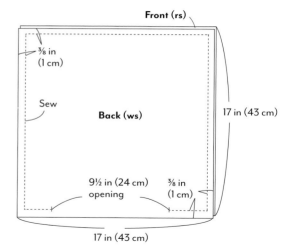

Front (rs)

⅜ in (1 cm)

Sew

Back (ws)

17 in (43 cm)

9½ in (24 cm) opening

⅜ in (1 cm)

17 in (43 cm)

4. Turn right side out through the opening. Insert the pillow form. Fold the opening seam allowances in, and then neatly hand stitch closed.

FULL-SIZE TEMPLATE

The numbers in parentheses indicate how many threads to remove and their spacing (1–3 means to remove one thread, leaving three threads).

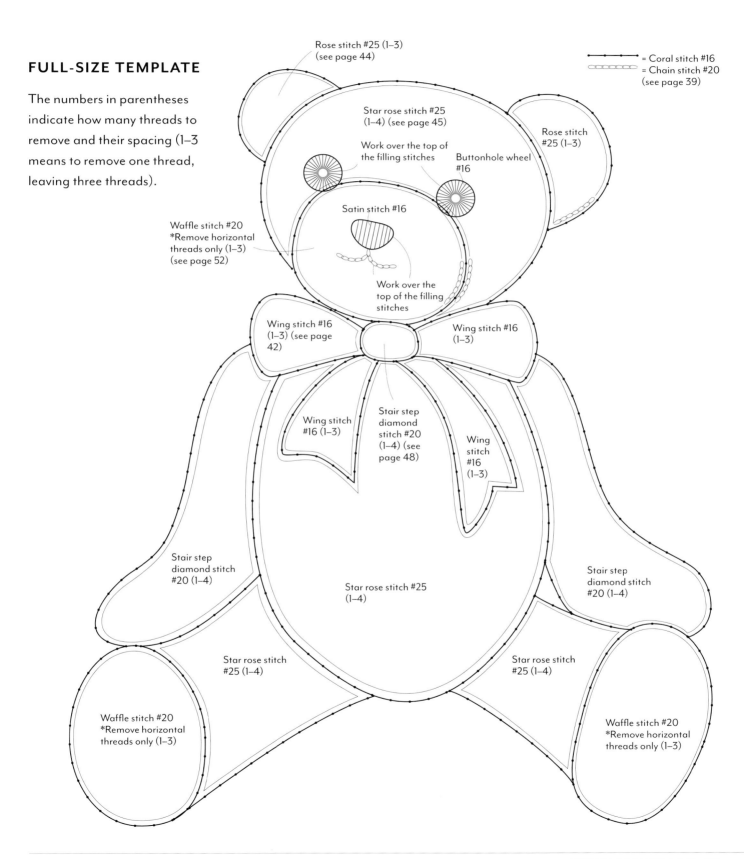

Rose stitch #25 (1–3) (see page 44)

= Coral stitch #16
= Chain stitch #20 (see page 39)

Star rose stitch #25 (1–4) (see page 45)

Work over the top of the filling stitches

Buttonhole wheel #16

Rose stitch #25 (1–3)

Satin stitch #16

Waffle stitch #20 *Remove horizontal threads only (1–3) (see page 52)

Work over the top of the filling stitches

Wing stitch #16 (1–3) (see page 42)

Wing stitch #16 (1–3)

Wing stitch #16 (1–3)

Stair step diamond stitch #20 (1–4) (see page 48)

Wing stitch #16 (1–3)

Stair step diamond stitch #20 (1–4)

Star rose stitch #25 (1–4)

Stair step diamond stitch #20 (1–4)

Star rose stitch #25 (1–4)

Star rose stitch #25 (1–4)

Waffle stitch #20 *Remove horizontal threads only (1–3)

Waffle stitch #20 *Remove horizontal threads only (1–3)

Hen Pillow

Shown on page 17

MATERIALS

> Linen fabric: 28 count in white
  – 37 x 24½ in (94 x 62 cm)
> Thread: Six-strand embroidery floss
in white (3865)
  – #25: 2 skeins
> 18 x 14 in (45.5 x 35.5 cm) pillow
form

FINISHED SIZE

15¾ x 12 in (40 x 30)

FULL-SIZE TEMPLATE

Pattern Sheet B

INSTRUCTIONS

1. Cut one 16½ in (42 cm) square of fabric for the front and one 16½ x 12¾ in (42 x 32 cm) rectangle of fabric for the back.

2. Use the template on Pattern Sheet B to trace the design onto the center of the front fabric, then embroider as noted. Chain stitch with two strands for the outline and dividing lines, then use one strand for the filling stitches. When the embroidery is complete, trim the fabric into a 16½ x 12¾ in (42 x 32 cm) rectangle with the embroidery centered.

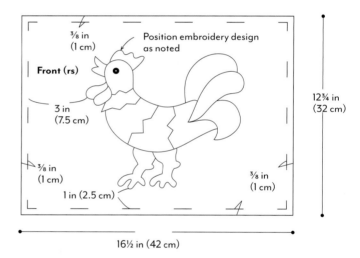

3. Cut two 15¾ x 2¼ in (40 x 5.5 cm) rectangles for the flanges. Buttonhole stitch the pyramids as noted in the Stitch Diagram on page 109. Each rectangle will have five pyramids. Next, trim the excess fabric away to reveal the pyramid shapes. Take care not to cut through the buttonhole stitches.

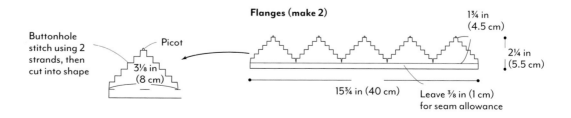

4. With right sides together, align the straight edges of the flanges with the top and bottom of the front from step 2. Align the back on top with the wrong side facing up. Sew, leaving a large opening in one side.

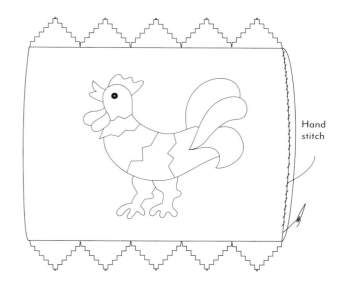

5. Turn right side out through the opening. Insert the pillow form. Fold the opening seam allowances in, and then neatly hand stitch closed.

STITCH DIAGRAM

Use 2 strands to sew buttonhole stitch as shown in the diagram below, then carefully trim the fabric away along the edge of the stitching.

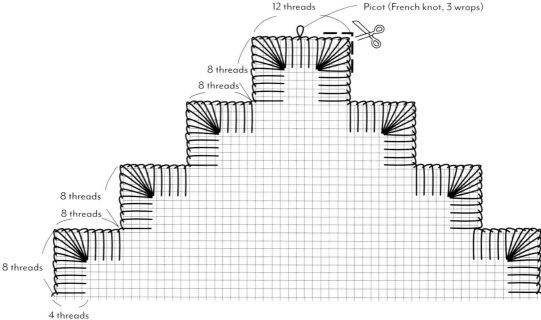

Drawn Thread Bolster

Shown on page 18

MATERIALS

> Linen fabric: 38 count in white
  - 28 x 32 in (71 x 81 cm) for pillow
  - Two 1¼ x 23¾ in (3 x 60 cm) bias strips for ruffles
> Thread: DMC coton a broder in white (B5200)
  - #20: 1 skein
  - #25: 1 skein
  - #30: 1 skein
> 6 x 14 in (15 x 35.5 cm) bolster pillow form

FINISHED SIZE

6 in (15 cm) in diameter x 14¼ in (36 cm) long without ruffles

FULL-SIZE TEMPLATE

Pattern Sheet B

INSTRUCTIONS

1. Cut a 20 x 24 in (51 x 61 cm) rectangle of fabric. Use the template on Pattern Sheet B to trace the design onto the center of the fabric, then embroider as noted. When the embroidery is complete, trim the fabric to 15 x 19 in (38 x 48 cm).

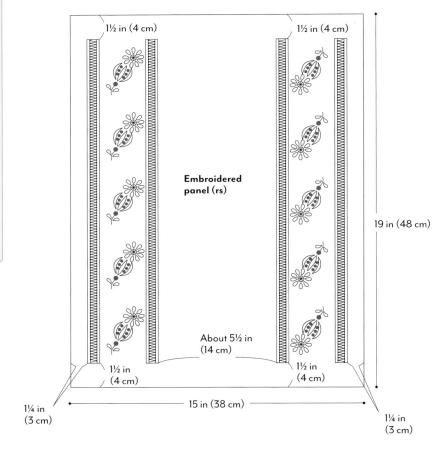

1½ in (4 cm)   1½ in (4 cm)

Embroidered panel (rs)

19 in (48 cm)

About 5½ in (14 cm)

1½ in (4 cm)   1½ in (4 cm)

1¼ in (3 cm)

15 in (38 cm)

1¼ in (3 cm)

2. Cut two 1¼ x 23¾ in (3 x 60 cm) bias strips. To make the ruffles, fold each bias strip in half along the full length. Use a long stitch length to sew along the raw edges, then pull the thread tails to gather the ruffles to a length of 19 in (48 cm). Next, align the raw edges of the ruffles with the left and right edges of the embroidered panel, so they run parallel to the drawn thread work. Sew in place using ⅜ in (1 cm) seam allowance. Finally, fold the embroidered panel in half with right sides together to form a tube. Sew, then turn right side out.

3. Insert the pillow form into the tube. Cut two 6¾ in (17 cm) diameter circles for the gussets. Fold and press the seam allowance over ⅜ in (1 cm) to the wrong side. Hand stitch the gussets in place on the ends of the tube. You will be stitching the gussets to the ruffles.

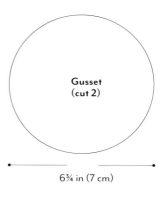

Gusset
(cut 2)

6¾ in (7 cm)

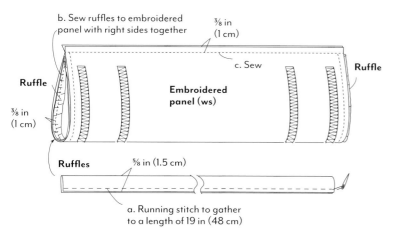

b. Sew ruffles to embroidered panel with right sides together

⅜ in (1 cm)

c. Sew

Ruffle

Ruffle

Embroidered panel (ws)

⅜ in (1 cm)

Ruffles

⅝ in (1.5 cm)

a. Running stitch to gather to a length of 19 in (48 cm)

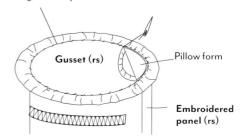

Fold and press seam allowances under, then hand stitch gussets in place

Gusset (rs)

Pillow form

Embroidered panel (rs)

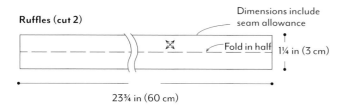

Ruffles (cut 2)

Dimensions include seam allowance

Fold in half

1¼ in (3 cm)

23¾ in (60 cm)

Broderie Anglaise Cushion

Shown on page 18

MATERIALS

> Linen fabric: Finely woven fabric in white
  - 38 x 19 in (96.5 x 48.5 cm) for pillow front and back
  - 2⅜ x 71 in (6 x 180 cm) for ruffle
> Thread: DMC coton a broder in white (B5200)
  - #16: 1 skein
  - #25: 2 skeins
> 15 in (38 cm) round pillow form
> 57 in (144 cm) of ¼ in (6 mm) wide white satin ribbon

FINISHED SIZE

12¼ in (31 cm) in diameter without ruffles

FULL-SIZE TEMPLATES

Pattern Sheet B

INSTRUCTIONS

1. Cut a 19 in (48.5 cm) square of fabric for the front. Use the template on Pattern Sheet B to trace the design onto the center of the fabric, then embroider as noted. When the embroidery is complete, trim the fabric into a circle following the seam allowance line noted on the template.

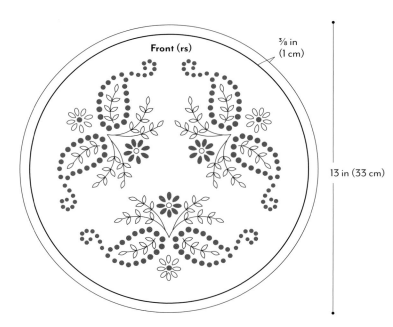

Front (rs)

⅜ in (1 cm)

13 in (33 cm)

2. Cut a 2⅜ x 71 in (6 x 180 cm) rectangle for the ruffle. Use a long stitch length to sew along one of the long edges. Pull the thread tails to gather the ruffle to a length of 41¾ in (106 cm). Set aside.

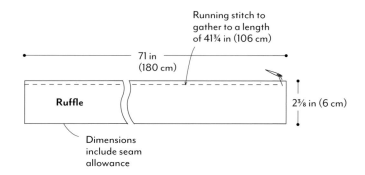

Running stitch to gather to a length of 41¾ in (106 cm)

71 in (180 cm)

Ruffle

2⅜ in (6 cm)

Dimensions include seam allowance

3. Use the templates on Pattern Sheet B to cut backs A and B out of fabric. Finish the straight edges and attach the ribbons as shown below.

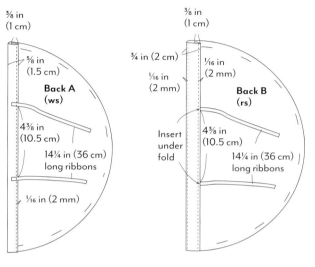

⅜ in (1 cm)

⅝ in (1.5 cm)

Back A (ws)

4⅜ in (10.5 cm)

14¼ in (36 cm) long ribbons

1/16 in (2 mm)

Fold straight edge over twice and topstitch with ribbons on top

⅜ in (1 cm)

¾ in (2 cm)

1/16 in (2 mm)

1/16 in (2 mm)

Insert under fold

Back B (rs)

4⅜ in (10.5 cm)

14¼ in (36 cm) long ribbons

Fold straight edge over twice, insert ribbons under fold, and topstitch

4. With right sides together, align the gathered edge of the ruffle from step 2 with the embroidered front from step 1. Overlap the short ends as shown below. Next, with right sides together, align backs A and B with the front. Back B will overlap back A. Sew together around the circle.

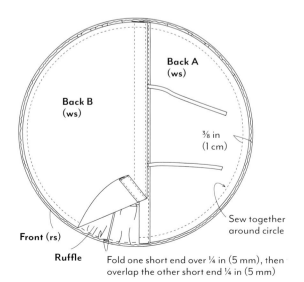

Back A (ws)

Back B (ws)

⅜ in (1 cm)

Sew together around circle

Front (rs)

Ruffle

Fold one short end over ¼ in (5 mm), then overlap the other short end ¼ in (5 mm)

5. Turn the pillow right side out. Insert the pillow form. Use the ribbon ties to secure in place on the back.

Front

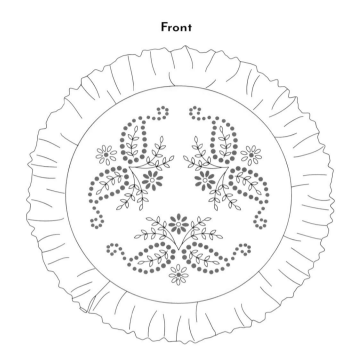

Back

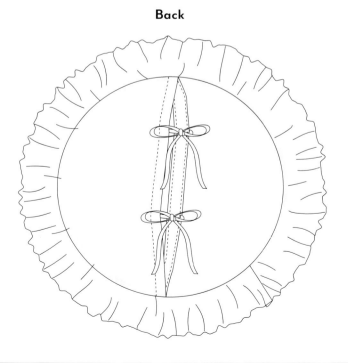

Envelope Pillow

Shown on page 19

MATERIALS

> Linen fabric: Finely woven fabric in white
  – 20 x 57½ in (51 x 146 cm)
> Thread: DMC coton a broder in white (B5200)
  – #20: 3 skeins
  – #25: 2 skeins
> 18 in (45 cm) square pillow form

FINISHED SIZE

16⅛ x 16⅛ in (41 x 41 cm)

FULL-SIZE TEMPLATE

Pattern Sheet A

INSTRUCTIONS

1. Use the template on Pattern Sheet A to trace the design onto the fabric. The design should be positioned at the top, but extra fabric is provided to allow the work to sit within a hoop. You should have at least 40¼ in (102 cm) of fabric beneath the area to be embroidered.

2. Embroider as noted, except the edging. Trim the scalloped edges of the flap into shape along the cutting lines, which include seam allowance. Fold and press the scalloped edges over ⅜ in (1 cm) to the wrong side, clipping the curves where necessary. Complete the needlelace edging as noted on the template. If necessary, trim the rest of the fabric into shape following the dimensions shown at right.

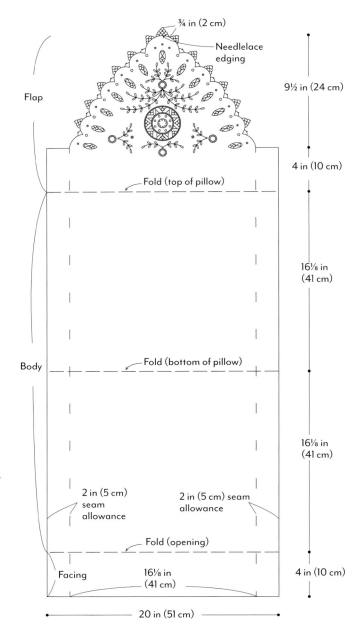

3. Fold and press the bottom edge over 4 in (10 cm) to the wrong side to create the facing. Next, fold the bottom portion of the pillow with right sides together so it measures 16⅛ in (41 cm). Sew together along the sides of the pillow using 2 in (5 cm) seam allowance.

4. Turn the pillow right side out. Insert the pillow form. Fold the flap down over the front of the pillow.

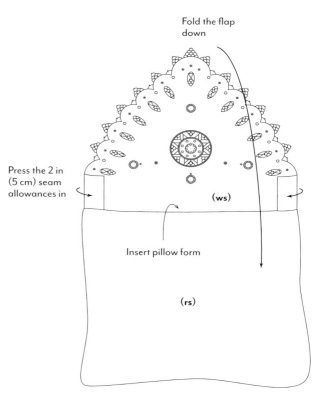

(rs)

Facing 4 in (10 cm)

Opening

Sew

2 in
(5 cm)

2 in
(5 cm)

(ws)

Bottom
fold

Fold the flap
down

Press the 2 in
(5 cm) seam
allowances in

(ws)

Insert pillow form

(rs)

Whitework Sampler II

Shown on page 20

MATERIALS

> Linen fabric: 28 count in unbleached white
  - 17¾ x 17¾ in (45 x 45 cm)
> Thread: Six-strand embroidery floss in ECRU
  - #25: 1 skein

FINISHED SIZE

12 x 12 in (30 x 30 cm)

INSTRUCTIONS

1. Mark a 12 in (30 cm) square on the linen fabric. This will be the finished size of the sample. Remove a thread ¾ in (2 cm) from the marked line along each side and work one-sided hem stitch along the edges (refer to page 118 for one-sided hem stitch instructions).

2. Work the pulled thread embroidery as shown in the diagrams below and on page 117.

3. Trim the fabric into a 14¼ in (36 cm) square. Fold and press the raw edges over ⅜ in (1 cm), then ¾ in (2 cm), mitering the corners as shown in the guide on page 145. Hand stitch the hem in place on the wrong side of the sampler.

SAMPLER OVERVIEW DIAGRAM

Use one strand of #25 embroidery floss.

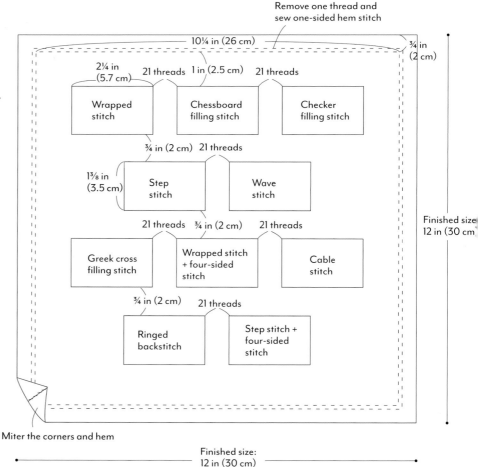

Remove one thread and sew one-sided hem stitch

10¼ in (26 cm)

¾ in (2 cm)

2¼ in (5.7 cm) 21 threads 1 in (2.5 cm) 21 threads

| Wrapped stitch | Chessboard filling stitch | Checker filling stitch |

¾ in (2 cm) 21 threads

1⅜ in (3.5 cm)

| Step stitch | Wave stitch |

21 threads ¾ in (2 cm) 21 threads

| Greek cross filling stitch | Wrapped stitch + four-sided stitch | Cable stitch |

¾ in (2 cm) 21 threads

| Ringed backstitch | Step stitch + four-sided stitch |

Finished size 12 in (30 cm)

Miter the corners and hem

Finished size: 12 in (30 cm)

EMBROIDERY DIAGRAMS

Wrapped Stitch
(see page 84)

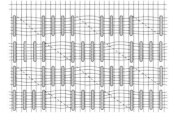

Chessboard Filling Stitch
(see page 84)

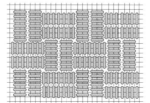

Checker Filling Stitch
(see page 85)

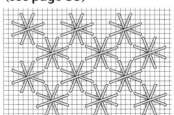

Step Stitch (see page 85)

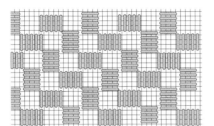

Wave Stitch (see page 85)

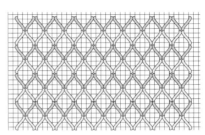

Greek Cross Filling Stitch
(see page 86)

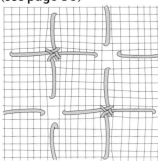

Wrapped Stitch + Four-Sided Stitch (see page 86)

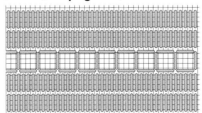

Cable Stitch (see page 87)

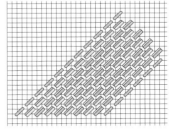

Ringed Backstitch
(see page 87)

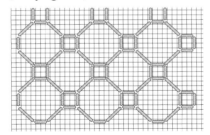

Step Stitch + Four-Sided Stitch
(see page 87)

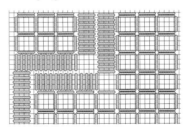

One-Sided Hem Stitch

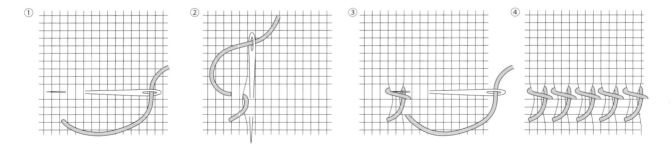

Where the thread has been removed, take the needle under the same number of threads (three are shown here) for the vertical and horizontal stitches.

Christening Gown

Shown on page 22

INSTRUCTIONS

1. Templates are included for the sleeve and bodice pieces, but you'll need to draft your own for the skirt pieces. Use the diagrams below and on page 120 to draft patterns for the skirt front, skirt back, skirt front lining, and skirt back lining.

Skirt Front

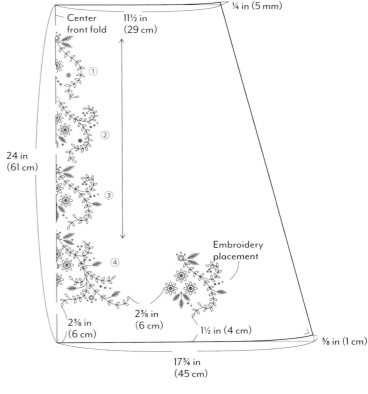

Center front fold · 11½ in (29 cm) · ¼ in (5 mm) · 24 in (61 cm) · ① ② ③ ④ · Embroidery placement · 2⅜ in (6 cm) · 2⅜ in (6 cm) · 1½ in (4 cm) · ⅜ in (1 cm) · 17¾ in (45 cm)

Skirt Back

6½ in (16.5 cm) · 10¼ in (26 cm) · ¼ in (5 mm) · 24 in (61 cm) · End of seam · Center back · Embroidery placement · 3½ in (9 cm) · 2⅜ in (6 cm) · ⅜ in (1 cm) · 16½ in (42 cm)

Skirt Front Lining

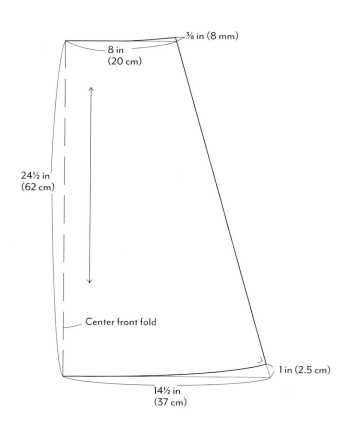

⅜ in (8 mm)

8 in (20 cm)

24½ in (62 cm)

Center front fold

1 in (2.5 cm)

14½ in (37 cm)

Skirt Back Lining

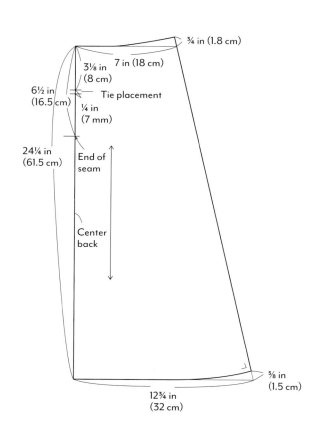

¾ in (1.8 cm)

7 in (18 cm)

3⅛ in (8 cm)

6½ in (16.5 cm)

Tie placement

¼ in (7 mm)

24¼ in (61.5 cm)

End of seam

Center back

12¾ in (32 cm)

⅝ in (1.5 cm)

2. Trace and cut out the templates on Pattern Sheet A. Arrange these templates, plus the ones drafted in step 1, on the fabric following the Cutting Diagram on page 121. Measure and mark the seam allowance for the skirt pieces as noted in the diagram (seam allowance is already included for the sleeve and bodice pieces). You'll also need to cut six ties on the bias, as noted in the diagram on page 121 (do not add seam allowance to the ties). Cut the pieces out of the fabric. When cutting out the skirt front, skirt backs, and bodice front, make sure to cut oversized fabric pieces as these will be embroidered—they will be trimmed into shape later.

Tie (cut on bias without seam allowance)

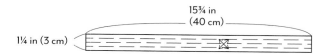

15¾ in (40 cm)

1¼ in (3 cm)

CUTTING DIAGRAM

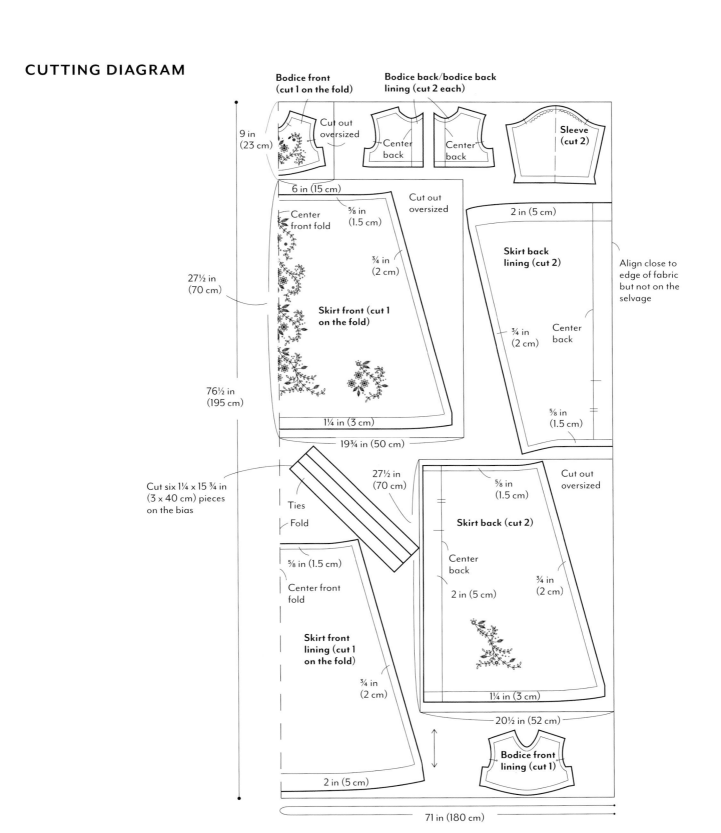

Bodice front
(cut 1 on the fold)

Bodice back/bodice back lining (cut 2 each)

Cut out oversized

Center back

Center back

Sleeve (cut 2)

9 in (23 cm)

6 in (15 cm)

Center front fold

⅝ in (1.5 cm)

Cut out oversized

2 in (5 cm)

Skirt back lining (cut 2)

Align close to edge of fabric but not on the selvage

¾ in (2 cm)

27½ in (70 cm)

Skirt front (cut 1 on the fold)

¾ in (2 cm)

Center back

76½ in (195 cm)

⅝ in (1.5 cm)

1¼ in (3 cm)

19¾ in (50 cm)

Cut six 1¼ x 15¾ in (3 x 40 cm) pieces on the bias

27½ in (70 cm)

⅝ in (1.5 cm)

Cut out oversized

Ties

Fold

Skirt back (cut 2)

⅝ in (1.5 cm)

Center front fold

Center back

2 in (5 cm)

Skirt front lining (cut 1 on the fold)

¾ in (2 cm)

¾ in (2 cm)

1¼ in (3 cm)

20½ in (52 cm)

2 in (5 cm)

Bodice front lining (cut 1)

71 in (180 cm)

3. Use the motifs on Pattern Sheet A to trace the embroidery designs onto the skirt front, skirt backs, and bodice front. For the skirt front, you'll need to align the four portions of the motif as noted on the pattern sheet to create the complete motif (also refer to the step 1 diagram on page 119). Embroider as noted, except for any edging. Trim the embroidered pieces into shape along the seam allowance lines.

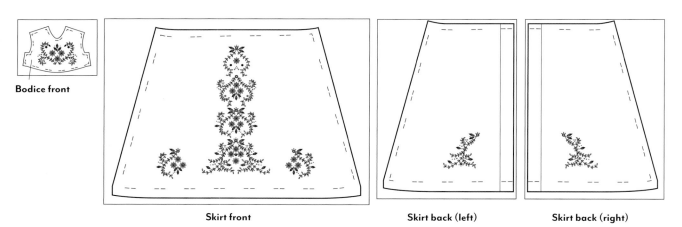

Bodice front

Skirt front

Skirt back (left)

Skirt back (right)

4. Make the ties: Fold and press one short end of each tie over ⅜ in (1 cm) to the wrong side. Next, fold and press each long end over ¼ in (5 mm) to the wrong side. Fold the tie in half, then topstitch along the edge. Make six ties total.

Make 6 ties

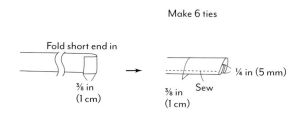

Fold short end in

⅜ in
(1 cm)

⅜ in
(1 cm)

Sew

¼ in (5 mm)

5. Sew the skirt with French seams: With wrong sides together, sew a skirt back piece to each flared edge of the skirt front using ¼ in (5 mm) seam allowance. Trim the seam allowances, then fold the skirt with right sides together. Sew along the flared edges of the skirt again, taking a slightly larger seam allowance of ½ in (1.5 cm) this time. This will conceal the raw edges and create a neatly finished seam. Follow the same process to sew the skirt lining.

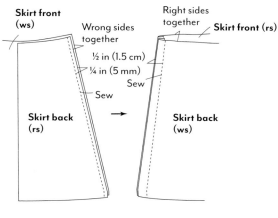

Skirt front
(ws)

Wrong sides
together

Right sides
together

Skirt front (rs)

½ in (1.5 cm)

¼ in (5 mm)

Sew

Sew

Skirt back
(rs)

Skirt back
(ws)

Repeat for skirt lining

6. Gather the waist: Use a long stitch length to baste two rows of gathering stitches along the waist of the skirt, as shown below. Pull the thread tails to gather the skirt. Follow the same process to gather the skirt lining.

¼ in (7 mm) ½ in (1.2 cm)

Baste two rows, then pull thread tails

⅝ in (1.5 cm)

Skirt

Repeat for skirt lining

7. Hem the skirt and sew the center back seam: Fold and press the skirt hem over 1 in (2.5 cm) to the wrong side twice. Hand stitch the hem in place on the inside of the garment. Next, use 2 in (5 cm) seam allowance to sew the two skirt back pieces with right sides together, stopping at the end of seam mark. Press the seam open. Fold and press each seam allowance under ¾ in (2 cm), then topstitch the fold in place, sewing through the seam allowance only (not the skirt) to finish the seam.

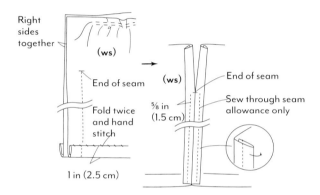

Right sides together

(ws)

End of seam

Fold twice and hand stitch

1 in (2.5 cm)

(ws)

⅝ in (1.5 cm)

End of seam

Sew through seam allowance only

8. Sew the skirt lining: Follow the same process used in step 7 to hem the skirt lining. Next, sew Hedebo buttonhole stitch on the folded edge of the hem, stopping 2 in (5 cm) from each end, then sew the edging motif as noted on page 125. Next, use 2 in (5 cm) seam allowance to sew the two skirt back lining pieces with right sides together, stopping at the end of seam mark. Press the seam open. Topstitch each seam allowance about ¼ in (5 mm) from the edge, sewing through the seam allowance only. Finally, sew a tie to each seam allowance following the placement noted in the diagram on page 120.

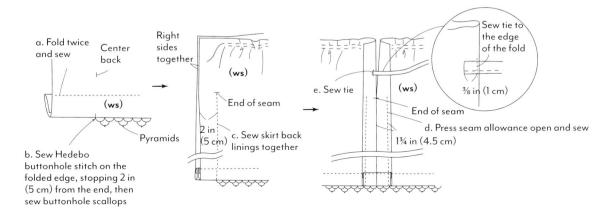

a. Fold twice and sew Center back

Right sides together

(ws)

(ws)

b. Sew Hedebo buttonhole stitch on the folded edge, stopping 2 in (5 cm) from the end, then sew buttonhole scallops

Pyramids

End of seam

2 in (5 cm)

c. Sew skirt back linings together

e. Sew tie

(ws)

End of seam

1¾ in (4.5 cm)

Sew tie to the edge of the fold

⅜ in (1 cm)

d. Press seam allowance open and sew

9. Make the sleeves: Use a long stitch length to sew two rows of gathering stitches along the curved edge of each sleeve (refer to template for placement). Pull the thread tails to gather the sleeves. Next, fold each sleeve in half with wrong sides together and sew using ¼ in (7 mm) seam allowance. Trim the seam allowances. Turn inside out and sew again, taking a slightly larger seam allowance of ⅜ in (8 mm) this time to produce a French seam.

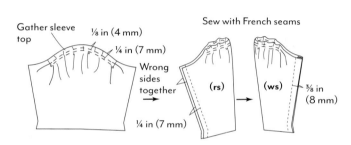

11. Sew the bodice with French seams: With wrong sides together, sew the bodice backs to the bodice front along the sides and shoulders using ¼ in (7 mm) seam allowance. Trim the seam allowances, then fold the bodice with right sides together. Sew along the sides and shoulders again, taking a slightly larger seam allowance of ⅜ in (8 mm) this time. Follow the same process to sew the bodice lining.

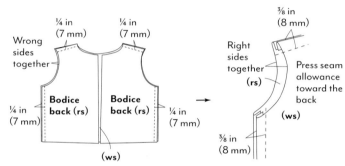

Repeat for bodice lining

10. Hem the sleeves: Fold and press the hems over ¼ in (5 mm) to the wrong side, then another ½ in (1.5 cm). Topstitch two rows, leaving a ⅜ in (1 cm) opening. Use the opening to insert a 4 in (10 cm) long piece of elastic through each casing. Sew the ends of the elastic together, then hand stitch the openings closed. Sew Hedebo buttonhole stitch on the folded edge of the sleeve hems, then sew the edging motif as noted on page 125.

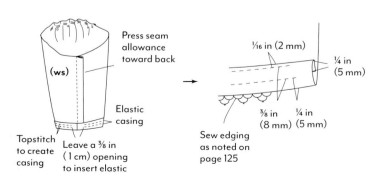

12. Sew the sleeves to the bodice: Align each sleeve with the bodice with right sides together, matching up the alignment marks. Adjust the gathers as necessary to make the sleeves fit the armholes. Sew together around the armholes using ⅜ in (1 cm) seam allowance.

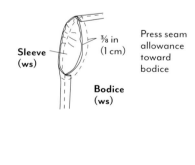

13. Sew the bodice and skirt together: Align the bodice and skirt with right sides together. Adjust the gathers as necessary to make the skirt fit the bodice, then sew to attach. Follow the same process to sew the bodice lining and skirt lining together.

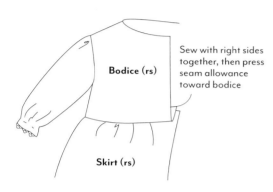

Sew with right sides together, then press seam allowance toward bodice

Bodice (rs)

Skirt (rs)

Repeat with bodice lining and skirt lining

14. Finish the dress: Sew the remaining four ties to the bodice lining using the process shown in step 8. Align the lining and dress with wrong sides together. Hand stitch the two together around the neckline and down the center back opening. Make sure to hand stitch the two together at the armholes as well. Sew Hedebo buttonhole stitch along the neckline, then sew the edging motif as noted in the diagram at right.

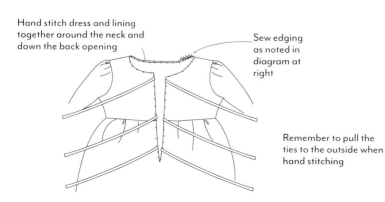

Hand stitch dress and lining together around the neck and down the back opening

Sew edging as noted in diagram at right

Remember to pull the ties to the outside when hand stitching

EDGING MOTIFS

Skirt Lining Hem Edging

Use coton a broder #30.

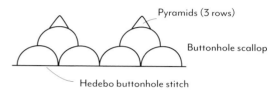

Pyramids (3 rows)

Buttonhole scallop

Hedebo buttonhole stitch

Sleeve Cuff Edging

Use coton a broder #30.

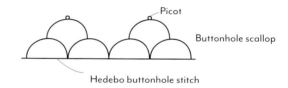

Picot

Buttonhole scallop

Hedebo buttonhole stitch

Neckline Edging

Use coton a broder #30.

Pyramids (3 rows)

Hedebo buttonhole stitch

Bundle of Joy Layette

Shown on page 24

MATERIALS (FOR THE BONNET)

> Linen fabric: Finely woven fabric in white
  − 31½ x 12¾ in (80 x 32 cm)
> Thread: DMC coton a broder in white (B5200)
  − #20: 1 skein
  − #25: 1 skein
> 31½ in (80 cm) of ¼ in (6 mm) wide satin ribbon

FINISHED SIZE

13½ in (34 cm) around the face and 5¾ in (14.5 cm) deep

FULL-SIZE TEMPLATES

Pattern Sheet B

INSTRUCTIONS

1. Cut a 17¾ x 9¾ in (45 x 25 cm) rectangle of fabric for the brim. Use the template on Pattern Sheet B and the Stitch Guide on page 128 to trace the cutting lines and embroidery design onto the brim so that the long curve touches the edge of the fabric. Embroider as noted, except the edging. Trim the brim into shape along the cutting lines (which include seam allowance). Fold and press the scalloped edge over ¼ in (7 mm) to the wrong side, clipping the curves where necessary. Complete the needlelace edging as noted in the Stitch Guide. Finally, sew running stitch in the seam allowance of the long curved edge of the brim. Leave long thread tails.

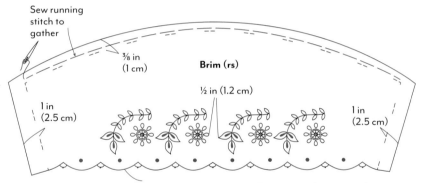

Sew running stitch to gather

⅜ in (1 cm)

Brim (rs)

½ in (1.2 cm)

1 in (2.5 cm)

1 in (2.5 cm)

Fold and press the seam allowance to the wrong side and sew the edging on the folded ege

2. Cut two 8 x 9¾ in (20 x 25 cm) rectangles for the outside gusset and inside gusset. Use the template on Pattern Sheet B to trace the gusset cutting lines for both pieces and the embroidery design for the outside gusset. Embroider the outside gusset as noted. Trim both pieces into shape along the cutting lines (which include seam allowance).

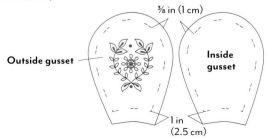

⅜ in (1 cm)

Outside gusset

Inside gusset

1 in (2.5 cm)

3. Pull the thread tails to gather the brim to match the size of the outside gusset, then sew with right sides together. Press the seam allowance toward the gusset.

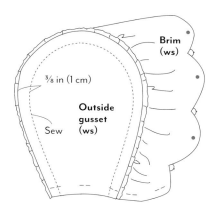

5. Fold and press the bottom edge of the bonnet over ⅜ in (1 cm) to the wrong side. Next, fold and press another ⅝ in (1.5 cm). Cut the ribbon in half, then sew each piece to the wrong side of the brim following the placement shown below. The ribbon should be inserted between the folds of the hem. Finally, hand stitch the hem in place on the inside of the bonnet.

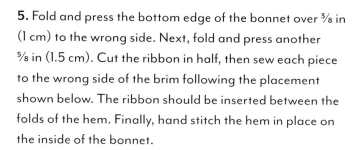

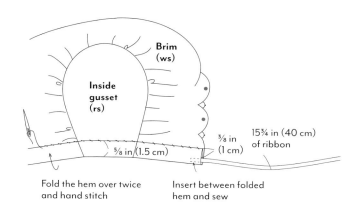

Fold the hem over twice and hand stitch

Insert between folded hem and sew

4. Fold and press the curved seam allowance of the inside gusset over ⅜ in (1 cm) to the wrong side. Hand stitch the inside gusset to the wrong side of the brim.

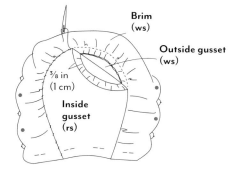

FINISHED DIAGRAM

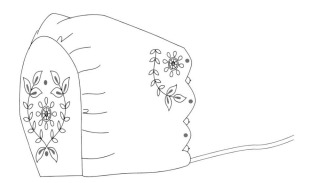

STITCH GUIDE FOR THE BONNET

— Use this to trace the embroidery design onto the fabric and to stitch. Use the template on Pattern Sheet B to mark the cutting lines and trim into shape.

— The brim design is symmetrical at the center line, except for the embroidery, which is repeated in the same orientation, not flipped. Move and trace again for the embroidery on the brim.

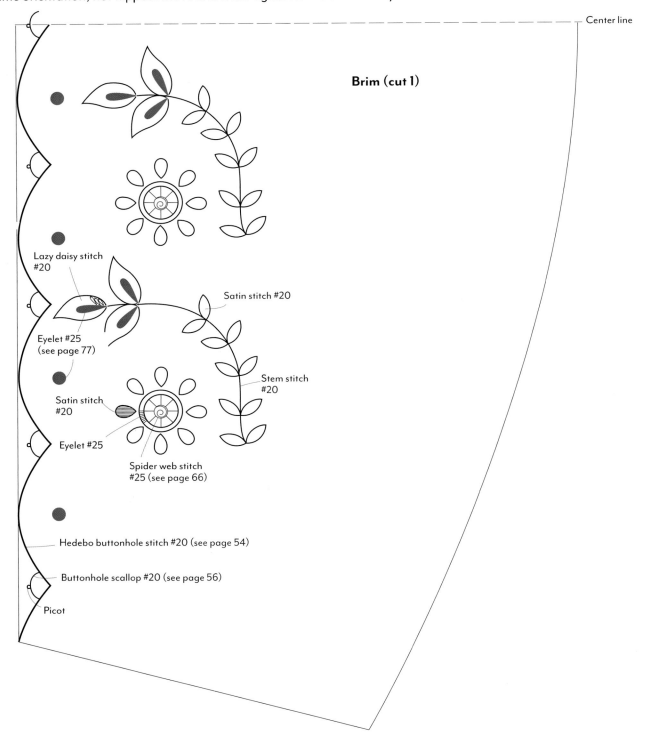

Center line

Brim (cut 1)

Lazy daisy stitch #20

Satin stitch #20

Eyelet #25 (see page 77)

Stem stitch #20

Satin stitch #20

Eyelet #25

Spider web stitch #25 (see page 66)

Hedebo buttonhole stitch #20 (see page 54)

Buttonhole scallop #20 (see page 56)

Picot

MATERIALS (FOR THE BOOTIES)

> Linen fabric: Finely woven fabric in white
  – 47¼ × 9¾ in (120 × 20 cm)
> Thread: DMC coton a broder in white (B5200)
  – #20: 1 skein
  – #25: 1 skein
> 28¼ in (72 cm) of ¼ in (6 mm) wide satin ribbon

FINISHED SIZE

4⅛ in (10.5 cm) from heel to toe

FULL-SIZE TEMPLATES

Pattern Sheet A

INSTRUCTIONS

1. Cut two 11¾ × 8 in (30 × 20 cm) rectangles of fabric for the sides. Use the template on Pattern Sheet A and the Stitch Guide on page 131 to trace the cutting lines and embroidery design onto the center of each piece. Embroider as noted, except the edging. Trim the sides into shape along the cutting lines (which include seam allowance). Fold and press the curved edge over ¼ in (7 mm) to the wrong side. Complete the needlelace edging as noted in the Stitch Guide.

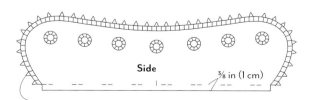

Fold and press the seam allowance to the wrong side and sew the edging on the folded ege

2. Cut two 8 in (20 cm) squares for the fronts. Use the template on Pattern Sheet A and the Stitch Guide on page 131 to trace the cutting lines and embroidery design onto the center of each piece. Embroider as noted, except the edging. Trim the fronts into shape along the cutting lines (which include seam allowance). Fold and press the top curved edge over ¼ in (7 mm) to the wrong side. Complete the needlelace edging as noted in the Stitch Guide.

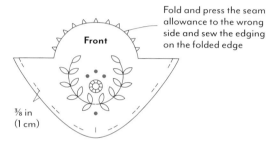

3. Use the template on Pattern Sheet A to cut two inner soles and two outer soles from the remaining fabric.

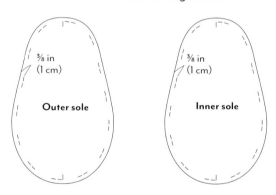

4. With right sides together, align each side with an outer sole, matching up marks noted on the template, and sew.

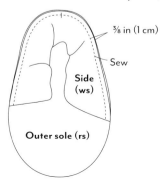

5. With right sides together, align each front with a piece from step 4, matching up marks noted on the template, and sew. Make sure that the seam allowances are pressed toward the sole.

7. Turn each shoe right side out. Cut the ribbon into four 7 in (18 cm) long pieces. Sew two pieces of ribbon to the wrong side of each shoe following the placement noted by ★s on the side template.

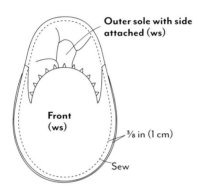

Outer sole with side attached (ws)

Front (ws)

⅜ in (1 cm)

Sew

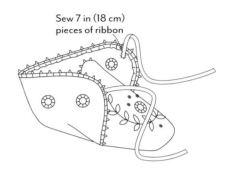

Sew 7 in (18 cm) pieces of ribbon

6. Fold and press the seam allowance over ⅜ in (1 cm) to the wrong side on the inner soles. Hand stitch an inner sole to the wrong side of each shoe.

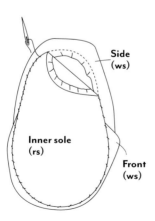

Side (ws)

Inner sole (rs)

Front (ws)

STITCH GUIDES FOR THE BOOTIES

Use this to trace the embroidery design onto the fabric and to stitch. Use the template on Pattern Sheet A to mark the cutting lines and trim into shape.

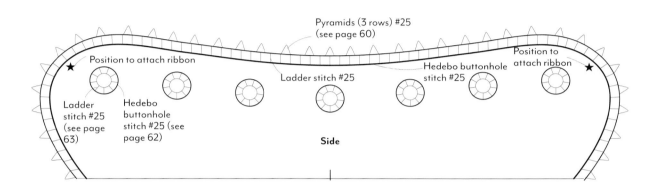

Pyramids (3 rows) #25 (see page 60)

Position to attach ribbon

Position to attach ribbon

Ladder stitch #25

Hedebo buttonhole stitch #25

Ladder stitch #25 (see page 63)

Hedebo buttonhole stitch #25 (see page 62)

Side

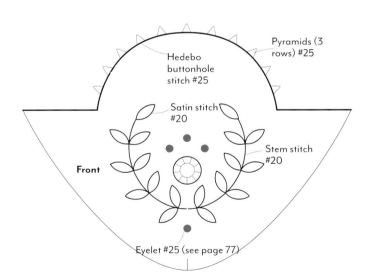

Pyramids (3 rows) #25

Hedebo buttonhole stitch #25

Satin stitch #20

Stem stitch #20

Front

Eyelet #25 (see page 77)

MATERIALS (FOR THE BIB)

> Linen fabric: Finely woven fabric in white
  – 21¾ x 13¾ in (55 x 35 cm)
  Thread: DMC coton a broder in white (B5200)
  – #20: 1 skein
  – #25: 1 skein
> 26¾ in (68 cm) of ¼ in (6 mm) wide satin ribbon

FINISHED SIZE

7½ in (19 cm) wide x 7 (18 cm) long

FULL-SIZE TEMPLATES

Pattern Sheet B

INSTRUCTIONS

1. Cut a 13¾ in (35 cm) square of fabric for the bib. Use the template on Pattern Sheet B and the Stitch Guide on page 133 to trace the cutting lines and embroidery design onto the center of the fabric. Embroider as noted, except the edging. Trim into shape along the cutting lines (which include seam allowance). Fold and press the seam allowance over ⅜ in (1 cm) to the wrong side on the outer curve only. Complete the needlelace edging as noted in the Stitch Guide.

2. Use the template on Pattern Sheet B to cut the lining from the remaining fabric. With right sides together, sew the bib and lining together around the neckline. Make clips into the seam allowance.

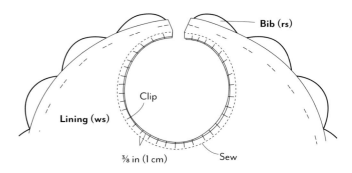

3. Turn the bib right side out. Fold and press the lining seam allowance over ⅜ in (1 cm) to the wrong side along the outer curve. Cut the ribbon in half. Insert the pieces of ribbon between the two layers of fabric and stitch in place so they are positioned at the back neck. Hand stitch the lining to the wrong side of the bib.

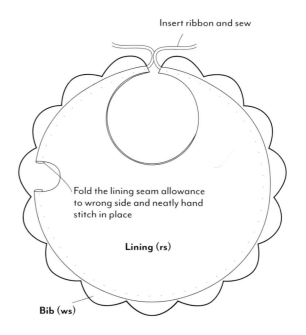

STITCH GUIDE FOR THE BIB

Use this to trace the embroidery
design onto the fabric and to
stitch. Use the template on
Pattern Sheet B to mark the
cutting lines and trim into shape.

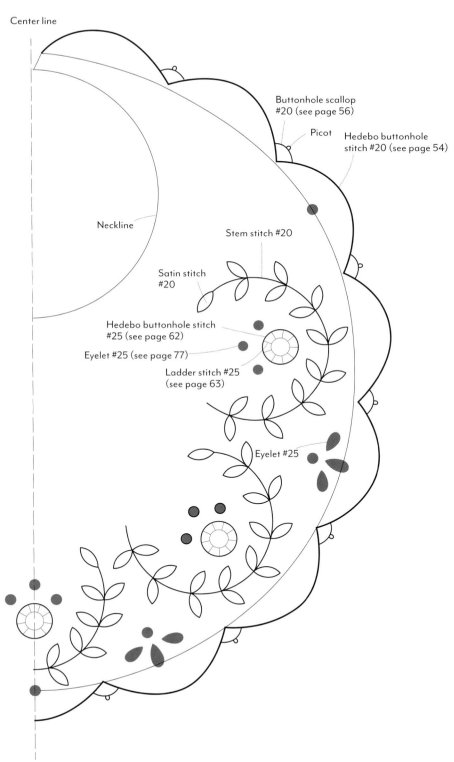

Center line

Buttonhole scallop
#20 (see page 56)

Picot

Hedebo buttonhole
stitch #20 (see page 54)

Neckline

Stem stitch #20

Satin stitch
#20

Hedebo buttonhole stitch
#25 (see page 62)

Eyelet #25 (see page 77)

Ladder stitch #25
(see page 63)

Eyelet #25

Scented Sachets

Shown on page 26

MATERIALS

> Linen fabric: 45 count in light cream or white
> - 14¼ x 6¼ in (36 x 16 cm) for the heart
> - 9¾ x 19¾ in (25 x 50 cm) for the rectangle
> - 11 x 19 in (28 x 48 cm) for the square
> Thread: DMC coton a broder in white (B5200)
> - #20: 1 skein
> - #25: 1 skein

FINISHED SIZES

Heart: 6¼ in (16 cm) wide x 6 in (15 cm) tall

Rectangle: 4 in (10 cm) wide x 5¼ in (13 cm) tall

Square: 5¼ in (13 cm) wide x 5¼ in (13 cm) tall

FULL-SIZE TEMPLATES

Pattern Sheet A

INSTRUCTIONS (FOR THE HEART)

1. Cut a 9¾ in (25 cm) square of fabric for the front. Use the template on Pattern Sheet A and the Stitch Guide on page 136 to trace the cutting lines and embroidery placement onto the center of the fabric. Trim into shape along the cutting lines (which include seam allowance). Fold and press the seam allowance over ⅜ in (1 cm) to the wrong side. Complete the needlelace edging around the outline and across the front of the heart as noted in the Stitch Guide.

2. Use the template on Pattern Sheet A to cut two symmetrical back pieces from the remaining fabric. Sew running stitch along the curved seam allowances. Pull the thread tails to help fold the curved seam allowance over ⅜ in (1 cm) to the wrong side. Fold and press the straight edges over ⅝ in (1.5 cm) to the wrong side.

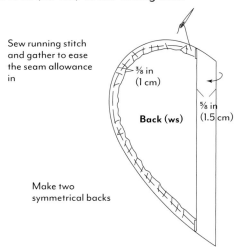

Sew running stitch and gather to ease the seam allowance in

⅜ in (1 cm)

Back (ws)

⅝ in (1.5 cm)

Make two symmetrical backs

3. Hand stitch the backs to the wrong side of the front along the curved edges. Hand stitch the two back pieces together for ¾ in (2 cm) at the top and bottom as shown below.

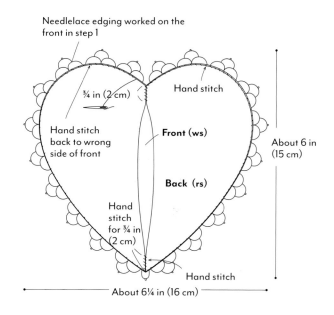

Needlelace edging worked on the front in step 1

¾ in (2 cm)

Hand stitch

Hand stitch back to wrong side of front

Front (ws)

Back (rs)

Hand stitch for ¾ in (2 cm)

Hand stitch

About 6 in (15 cm)

About 6¼ in (16 cm)

INSTRUCTIONS (FOR THE RECTANGLE AND SQUARE)

1. Use the template on Pattern Sheet A and the Stitch Guide on page 136 to trace the cutting lines and embroidery design onto the fabric so that the non-embroidered end of the pattern aligns with the edge of the fabric—this provides more fabric around the design for ease of embroidering. Mark the cutting lines for the bottom portion of the sachet using the dimensions provided in the diagrams below.

2. Embroider as noted, except the edging. Trim into shape along the cutting lines (which include seam allowance). Fold and press the flap edge seam allowance over ⅜ in (1 cm) to the wrong side, clipping the curves where necessary. Complete the needlelace edging as noted in the Stitch Guide.

3. Fold and press the bottom edge over ⅝ in (1.5 cm) to the wrong side. Next, fold the bottom portion of the sachet with right sides together so it measures 5¼ in (13.5 cm) for the rectangle or 5⅛ in (13 cm) for the square. Sew together along the sides of the sachet using ⅜ in (1 cm) seam allowance. Turn right side out. Fold the flap down to complete the rectangle sachet.

4. For the square sachet only, work two rows of Hedebo buttonhole stitch on the top layer of the sachet as shown in the diagram below. Carefully cut slits between the stitching to create the openings to insert the flap and complete the sachet.

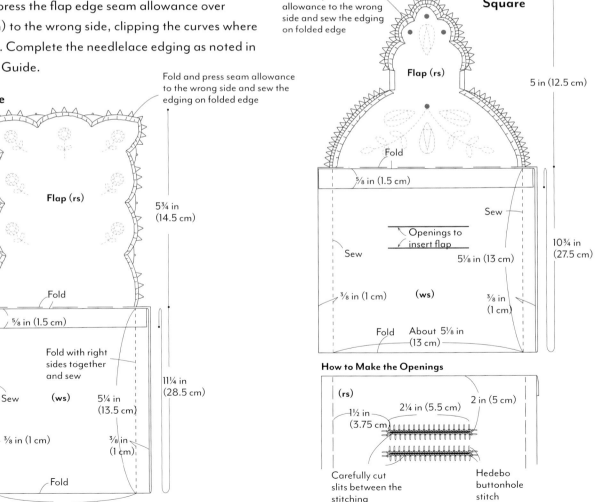

Rectangle

Fold and press seam allowance to the wrong side and sew the edging on folded edge

Flap (rs)

5¾ in (14.5 cm)

Fold

⅝ in (1.5 cm)

Fold with right sides together and sew

Sew   (ws)   5¼ in (13.5 cm)

⅜ in (1 cm)   ⅜ in (1 cm)

Fold

11¼ in (28.5 cm)

4 in (10 cm)

Square

Fold and press seam allowance to the wrong side and sew the edging on folded edge

Flap (rs)

5 in (12.5 cm)

Fold

⅝ in (1.5 cm)

Sew

Openings to insert flap

Sew   5⅛ in (13 cm)

⅜ in (1 cm)   (ws)   ⅜ in (1 cm)

Fold   About 5⅛ in (13 cm)

10¾ in (27.5 cm)

How to Make the Openings

(rs)

1½ in (3.75 cm)   2¼ in (5.5 cm)   2 in (5 cm)

Carefully cut slits between the stitching

Hedebo buttonhole stitch

STITCH GUIDES

Use these to trace the embroidery design onto the fabric and to stitch. Use the templates on Pattern Sheet A to mark the cutting lines and trim into shape.

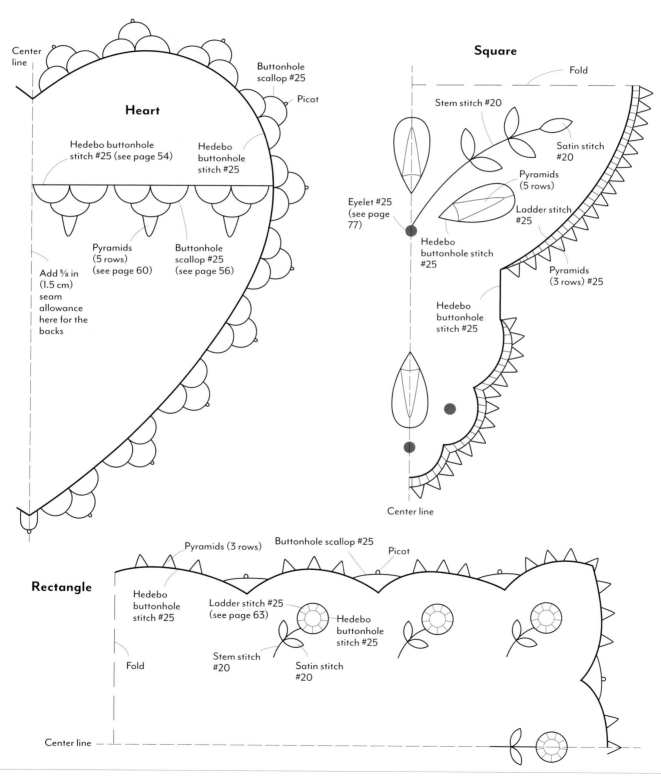

Center line

Heart

Buttonhole scallop #25

Picot

Hedebo buttonhole stitch #25 (see page 54)

Hedebo buttonhole stitch #25

Pyramids (5 rows) (see page 60)

Buttonhole scallop #25 (see page 56)

Add ⅝ in (1.5 cm) seam allowance here for the backs

Square

Fold

Stem stitch #20

Satin stitch #20

Pyramids (5 rows)

Eyelet #25 (see page 77)

Ladder stitch #25

Hedebo buttonhole stitch #25

Pyramids (3 rows) #25

Hedebo buttonhole stitch #25

Center line

Rectangle

Pyramids (3 rows)

Buttonhole scallop #25

Picot

Hedebo buttonhole stitch #25

Ladder stitch #25 (see page 63)

Hedebo buttonhole stitch #25

Stem stitch #20

Satin stitch #20

Fold

Center line

Modern Napkin Rings

Shown on page 31

MATERIALS (FOR ONE NAPKIN RING)

> Linen fabric: 30 count in light gray
  – 7 x 3⅛ in (18 x 8 cm)
> Thread: DMC coton a broder in white (B5200)
  – #16: 1 skein
> One ⅜ in (1 cm) diameter button

FINISHED SIZE

2 in (5 cm) wide x 6 in (15 cm) long

INSTRUCTIONS

1. Remove the threads at the specified positions and sew four-sided stitch.

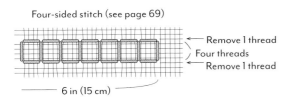

Four-sided stitch (see page 69)

Remove 1 thread
Four threads
Remove 1 thread

6 in (15 cm)

2. Fold and press the top and bottom seam allowances over ¼ in (5 mm) to the wrong side. Next, fold and press another ⅜ in (1 cm). Hand stitch in place on the wrong side.

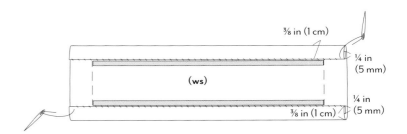

⅜ in (1 cm)

¼ in (5 mm)

(ws)

¼ in (5 mm)

⅜ in (1 cm)

3. Fold and press the left and right seam allowances over ¼ in (5 mm) to the wrong side. Next, fold and press another ⅜ in (1 cm). Hand stitch in place on the wrong side. Sew a buttonhole scallop at one end to create a button loop, then sew the button in the corresponding position on the other end.

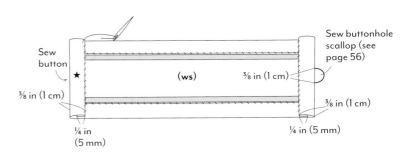

Sew button

Sew buttonhole scallop (see page 56)

⅜ in (1 cm)

(ws)

⅜ in (1 cm)

⅜ in (1 cm)

¼ in (5 mm)

¼ in (5 mm)

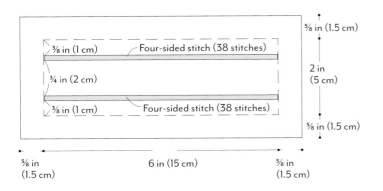

⅜ in (1 cm)

Four-sided stitch (38 stitches)

¾ in (2 cm)

⅜ in (1 cm)

Four-sided stitch (38 stitches)

⅝ in (1.5 cm)

2 in (5 cm)

⅝ in (1.5 cm)

⅝ in (1.5 cm)

6 in (15 cm)

⅝ in (1.5 cm)

Drawstring Pouches

Shown on page 27

MATERIALS

> Linen fabric: 55 count in white or light blue
  – 24 x 10¼ in (61 x 26 cm)
> Thread: DMC coton a broder in blue (800) or off-white (BLANC)
  – #25: 2 skeins
> Two 2¾ in (7 cm) diameter circles of felt

FINISHED SIZE

9¾ in (25 cm) wide x 8 in (20 cm) tall

INSTRUCTIONS

1. Cut a 20½ x 9 in (52 x 23 cm) rectangle of fabric for the body. Fold and press the top seam allowance over ⅜ in (1 cm) to the wrong side. Complete the needlelace edging as noted in the diagrams at right.

EDGING MOTIFS

White Pouch

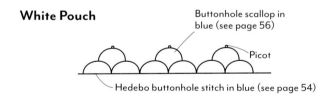

Buttonhole scallop in blue (see page 56)

Picot

Hedebo buttonhole stitch in blue (see page 54)

Blue Pouch

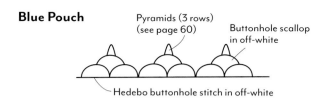

Pyramids (3 rows) (see page 60)

Buttonhole scallop in off-white

Hedebo buttonhole stitch in off-white

2. Cut a 20½ x 1 in (52 x 2.5 cm) rectangle of fabric for the drawstring casing. Fold and press the left and right edges ⅜ in (1 cm) to the wrong side. Next, fold and press the top and bottom edges over ¼ in (5 mm) to the wrong side. Topstitch the drawstring casing to the wrong side of the body following the placement noted in the step 1 diagram.

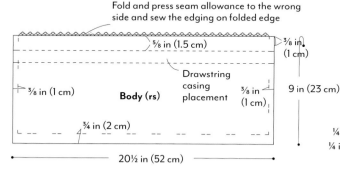

Fold and press seam allowance to the wrong side and sew the edging on folded edge

⅝ in (1.5 cm)

⅜ in (1 cm)

⅜ in (1 cm)

Body (rs)

Drawstring casing placement

⅜ in (1 cm)

9 in (23 cm)

¾ in (2 cm)

20½ in (52 cm)

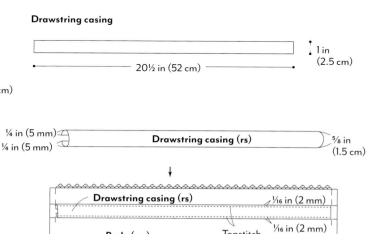

Drawstring casing

20½ in (52 cm)

1 in (2.5 cm)

¼ in (5 mm)

¼ in (5 mm)

Drawstring casing (rs)

⅝ in (1.5 cm)

Drawstring casing (rs)

1/16 in (2 mm)

Body (ws)

Topstitch

1/16 in (2 mm)

3. Fold the body in half with right sides together and sew the side seam, leaving a ⅝ in (1.5 cm) opening at the drawstring casing. Sew running stitch along the bottom seam allowance. Leave long thread tails.

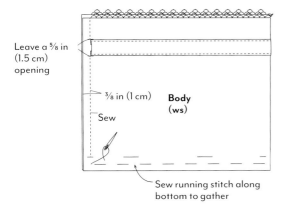

Leave a ⅝ in (1.5 cm) opening

⅜ in (1 cm)

Sew

Body (ws)

Sew running stitch along bottom to gather

4. Cut two 3½ in (9 cm) diameter circles of fabric for the bottom and bottom lining. Sew running stitch in the seam allowance of each piece, insert a felt circle, and gather, folding and pressing the seam allowance to the wrong side. Secure the gathering threads to complete the two padded bottoms.

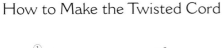

⅜ in (1 cm)

Bottom (cut 2)

3½ in (9 cm)

Felt circle (cut 2)

2¾ in (7 cm)

Cut without seam allowance

Bottom

Felt

Make 2 padded bottoms

Gather bottom seam allowance around felt

5. Pull the thread tails from step 3 to gather the pouch to match the size of the bottom. Hand stitch the bottom to the pouch body. Next, hand stitch the bottom lining to the inside of the pouch.

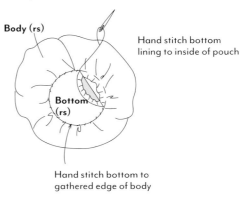

Body (rs)

Hand stitch bottom lining to inside of pouch

Bottom (rs)

Hand stitch bottom to gathered edge of body

6. Make the twisted cord as shown below, then insert through the drawstring casing to complete the pouch.

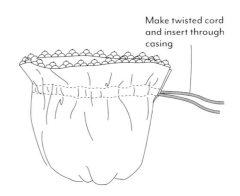

Make twisted cord and insert through casing

How to Make the Twisted Cord

White pouch: Blue thread
Blue pouch: Off-white thread

① Align about 2 yds (2 m) of 12 strands of thread. Twist in the same direction as the thread twist.

② Fold in half and twist in the opposite direction.

③ Tie a knot on both ends to secure the twist.

Ring Bearer Pillow

Shown on page 28

MATERIALS

> Linen fabric: 38 count in white
  – 54¾ x 8¾ in (139 x 22 cm)
> Thread: DMC coton a broder in off-white (BLANC)
  – #16: 2 skeins
  – #20: 5 skeins
  – #25: 1 skein
> 8 x 8 x 2 in (20 x 20 x 5 cm) foam pad
> 24¼ in (62 cm) of ⅛ in (3 mm) wide satin ribbon

FINISHED SIZE

8 x 8 in (20 x 20 cm) without edging

INSTRUCTIONS

1. Cut two 8¾ in (22 cm) squares of fabric. These will be the top and bottom.

2. Use the template on page 142 to trace the top embroidery design onto the center of the top fabric. Embroider as noted, except the edging. Fold and press the seam allowance over ⅜ in (1 cm) to the wrong side. Complete the needlelace edging as noted in the diagram below. Follow the same process to fold the seam allowance and work the needlelace edging on the bottom, making sure to work with the wrong side of the fabric facing up.

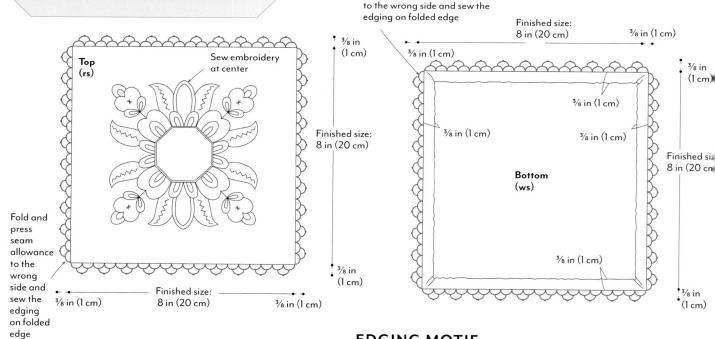

Top (rs)

Sew embroidery at center

Fold and press seam allowance to the wrong side and sew the edging on folded edge

⅜ in (1 cm)

Finished size: 8 in (20 cm)

⅜ in (1 cm)

Finished size: 8 in (20 cm)

⅜ in (1 cm)

Fold and press seam allowance to the wrong side and sew the edging on folded edge

Finished size: 8 in (20 cm)

⅜ in (1 cm)

⅜ in (1 cm)

⅜ in (1 cm)

⅜ in (1 cm)

⅜ in (1 cm)

Bottom (ws)

⅜ in (1 cm)

Finished size 8 in (20 cm)

⅜ in (1 cm)

EDGING MOTIF

*For the bottom, sew the edging with the wrong side facing up.

Picot

Buttonhole scallop (3 rows) #20 Work 10 motifs on each side of the pillow (see page 56)

Hedebo buttonhole stitch #20 (see page 54)

(rs)

3. Cut a 37½ x 8 in (95 x 20 cm) rectangle of fabric for the gusset. Mark a 32¼ x 2¾ in (82 x 7 cm) rectangle for the cutting lines (which include seam allowance), then mark to divide the rectangle into four equal sections. Use the template on page 143 to trace the gusset embroidery design onto the gusset fabric, positioning one pattern repeat at the center of each 8 in (20 cm) section. Embroider as noted. When the embroidery is complete, trim into shape along the cutting lines.

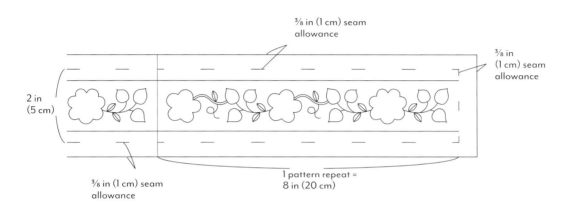

⅜ in (1 cm) seam allowance

⅜ in (1 cm) seam allowance

2 in (5 cm)

⅜ in (1 cm) seam allowance

1 pattern repeat = 8 in (20 cm)

4. Fold and press the gusset seam allowances over ⅜ in (1 cm) to the wrong side. Next, hand stitch the gusset to the wrong side of the pillow bottom. Hand stitch the two short ends of the gusset together where they meet at one of the corners. Insert the foam pad, then cover with the pillow top and hand stitch to the gusset.

5. Cut the ribbon in half. Sew the center of each piece of ribbon to the pillow following the placement noted on the top embroidery template. Make sure to sew through all the layers to the bottom of the pillow to create dimples. Secure the thread on the bottom of the pillow.

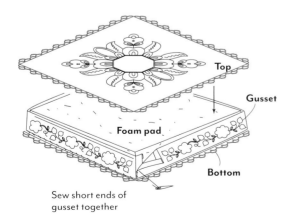

Top

Gusset

Foam pad

Bottom

Sew short ends of gusset together

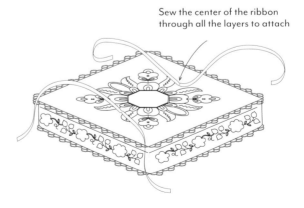

Sew the center of the ribbon through all the layers to attach

FULL-SIZE TEMPLATES

The numbers in parentheses indicate how many threads to remove and their spacing (1–3 means to remove one thread, leaving three threads).

Top Embroidery Design

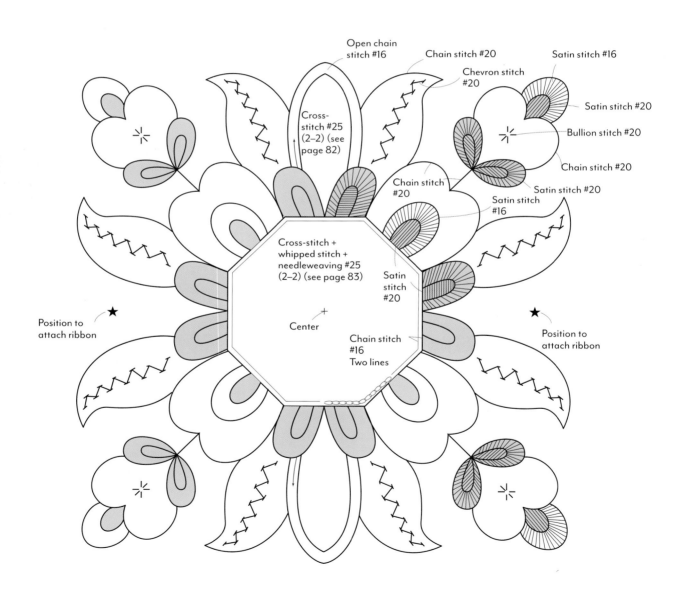

Open chain stitch #16

Chain stitch #20

Chevron stitch #20

Satin stitch #16

Satin stitch #20

Bullion stitch #20

Chain stitch #20

Satin stitch #20

Satin stitch #16

Cross-stitch #25 (2–2) (see page 82)

Chain stitch #20

Cross-stitch + whipped stitch + needleweaving #25 (2–2) (see page 83)

Satin stitch #20

Center

Position to attach ribbon

Position to attach ribbon

Chain stitch #16 Two lines

Gusset Embroidery Design

Trace this motif onto the center of each 8 in (20 cm) section.

Double wrap stitch #16 (see page 71)

*Don't remove any threads. Stitch along the entire 31½ in (80 cm) length of the gusset.

Center line

Chain stitch #20

Chain stitch #20

Chain stitch #20

Satin stitch #16

Cross-stitch + whipped stitch #25 (2–2) (see page 83)

Chain stitch #20

Satin stitch #20

Chain stitch #20

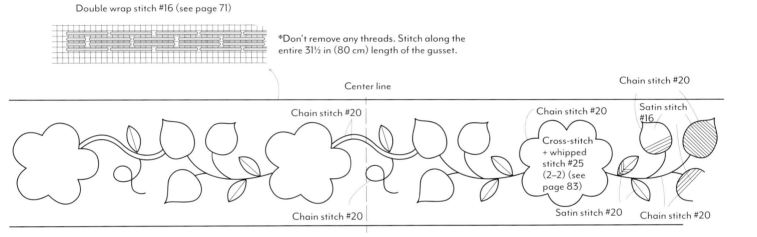

Everyday Table Runner

Shown on page 30

Shown on page 30

MATERIALS

> Linen fabric: 28 count in white
  – 22 x 18¼ in (56 x 46 cm)
> Thread: Six-strand embroidery floss
in ECRU
  – #25: 1 skein

FINISHED SIZE

13¾ x 9¾ in (35 x 25 cm)

INSTRUCTIONS

1. Mark a 13¾ x 9¾ in (35 x 25 cm) rectangle on the fabric. This represents the finished size of the table runner.

2. Sew a rectangle of four-sided stitch ¾ in (2 cm) in from the rectangle marked in step 1.

3. Work the four-sided stitch and step stitch design in each of the four corners of the rectangle, as noted in the Stitch Diagram on page 145.

4. Trim the embroidered fabric 1⅛ in (3 cm) outside the rectangle marked in step 1. Fold and press the raw edges over ⅜ in (1 cm), then ¾ in (2 cm), mitering the corners as shown in the guide on page 145. Hand stitch the hem in place on the wrong side of the table runner.

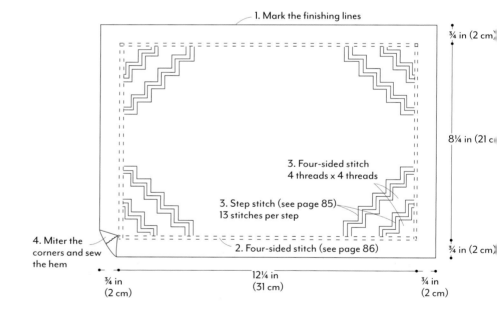

1. Mark the finishing lines

¾ in (2 cm)

8¼ in (21 cm)

3. Four-sided stitch
4 threads x 4 threads

3. Step stitch (see page 85)
13 stitches per step

4. Miter the corners and sew the hem

2. Four-sided stitch (see page 86)

¾ in (2 cm)

¾ in (2 cm)

12¼ in (31 cm)

¾ in (2 cm)

STITCH DIAGRAM

*Use one strand of #25 embroidery floss.

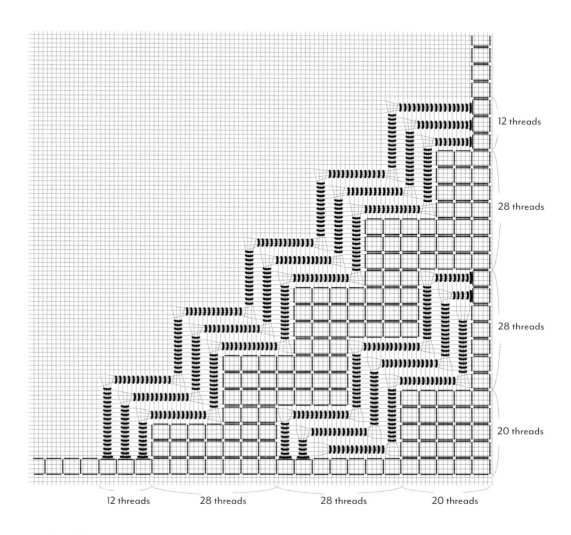

12 threads

28 threads

28 threads

20 threads

12 threads   28 threads   28 threads   20 threads

HOW TO MITER THE CORNERS

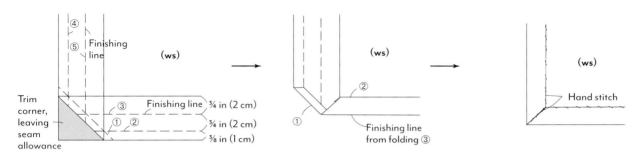

1. Trim the corners, leaving ⅜ in (1 cm) seam allowance from the finishing lines.

2. Fold and press the corner seam allowance in (①). Next, fold and press ②, then fold and press ③.

3. Fold and press ④ and ⑤. Hand stitch the folded edge to the wrong side of the fabric to secure the hem in place. Don't forget to hand stitch the corners together too.

Embroidery Tool Case

Shown on page 32

MATERIALS

> Linen fabric: 30 count in light gray
> – 29½ x 7¼ in (75 x 18.5 cm)
> Thread: Pearl cotton in ECRU
> – #12: 1 ball
> Fusible fleece: 9 x 6½ in (23 x 16.5 cm)
> One ½ in (1.3 cm) diameter button

FINISHED SIZE

9 x 6½ in (23 x 16.5 cm) when open

INSTRUCTIONS

1. From the linen, cut three 9¾ x 7¼ in (25 x 18.5 cm) pieces. Trim one of them down to 9¾ x 5 in (25 x 12.5 cm). This will be the pocket. The other two pieces will be the body outside and body lining.

2. Use the charts on page 148 to work the embroidery on the body outside and pocket (refer to the diagrams below for placement). Start from the center and work outward until there are 15 diamond motifs across on the body outside and 14 across on the pocket.

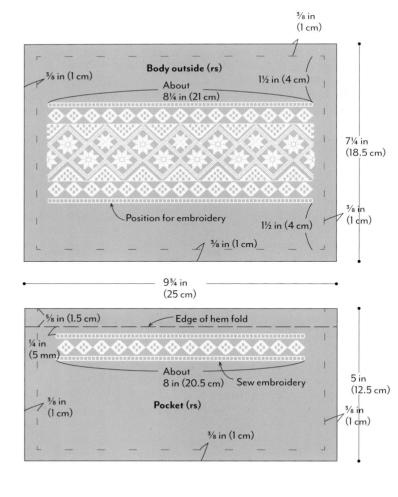

3. On the pocket's opening edge, fold and press ¼ in (5 mm) to the wrong side. Fold and press another ⅜ in (1 cm), and then hand stitch to secure the hem in place. Next, with right sides facing up, match the raw edges of the pocket with the body lining. Topstitch down the center of the pocket to attach.

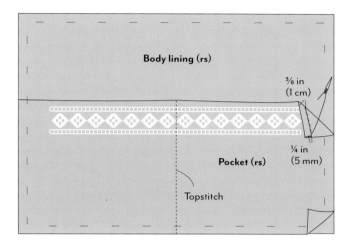

4. Adhere the fusible fleece to the wrong side of the body outside.

5. Align the body outside and body lining pieces with right sides together. Sew around the edge, leaving a 5½ in (14 cm) opening in the bottom edge.

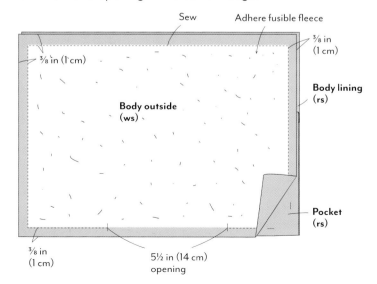

6. Turn right side out, fold the seam allowances in, and neatly hand stitch the opening to close it. On the outside of the case, sew a button loop at the left edge, and sew a button on the opposite edge to form a closure.

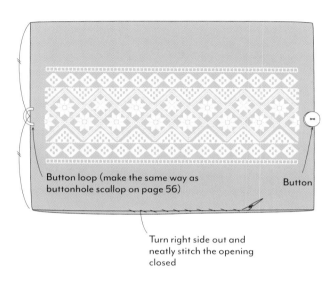

EMBROIDERY CHARTS

Body Outside

4 threads

Center

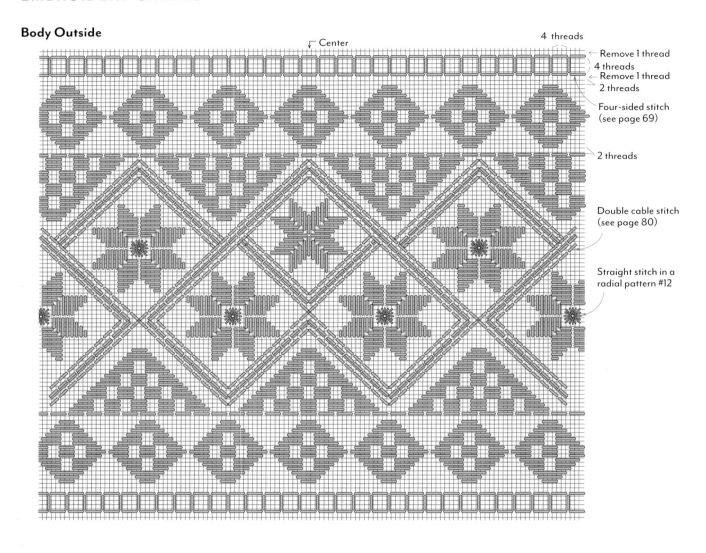

← Remove 1 thread
4 threads
← Remove 1 thread
2 threads

Four-sided stitch
(see page 69)

2 threads

Double cable stitch
(see page 80)

Straight stitch in a
radial pattern #12

Pocket

4 threads

Center

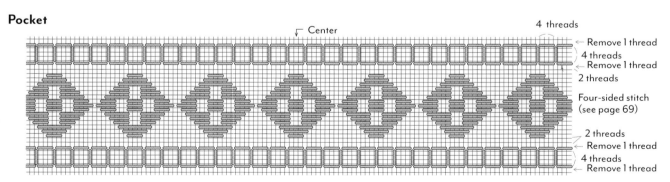

← Remove 1 thread
4 threads
← Remove 1 thread
2 threads

Four-sided stitch
(see page 69)

2 threads
← Remove 1 thread
4 threads
← Remove 1 thread

Buttonhole Scallop Coasters

Shown on page 11

MATERIALS

> Linen fabric: 28 count in white
  – 5¾ x 5¾ in (14.5 x 14.5 cm)
> Thread: DMC coton a broder in white
  (B5200), yellow (727), or light blue
  (800)
  – #16: 1 skein

FINISHED SIZE

5 x 5 in (12.5 x 12.5 cm)

INSTRUCTIONS

1. Cut a 5¾ in (14.5 cm) square of fabric.

2. Fold and press the edges over ⅜ in (1 cm) to the wrong side. Sew Hedebo buttonhole stitch on the folded edge, then complete the needlelace edging.

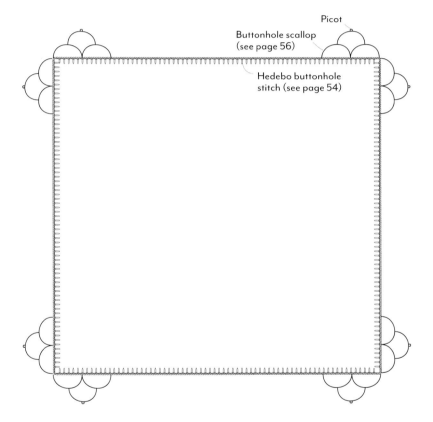

Picot

Buttonhole scallop
(see page 56)

Hedebo buttonhole
stitch (see page 54)

Cube Pincushions

Shown on page 34

Shown on page 34

MATERIALS (FOR ONE)

> Linen banding: 28 count in white
  – 17¼ x 2 in (44 x 5 cm)
> Thread: DMC coton a broder in
  unbleached white (ECRU), white
  (B5200), or light blue (775)
  – #25: 1 skein
> 2 in (5 cm) foam cube

FINISHED SIZE

2 x 2 x 2 in (5 x 5 x 5 cm)

INSTRUCTIONS

1. Cut the linen banding in half. Sew the desired needlelace edging on each piece of linen banding following the placement noted in the diagram.

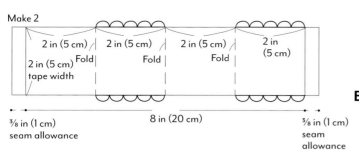

Make 2

2 in (5 cm)   2 in (5 cm)   2 in (5 cm)   2 in (5 cm)

2 in (5 cm) Fold   Fold   Fold
tape width

⅜ in (1 cm)   8 in (20 cm)   ⅜ in (1 cm)
seam allowance   seam allowance

2. Fold and press the short ends over ⅜ in (1 cm) to the wrong side. Fold one piece of linen banding into a square and hand stitch the short ends together where they meet at one of the corners.

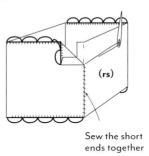

(rs)

Sew the short
ends together

3. Insert the foam cube. Wrap the other piece of linen banding around the foam cube and hand stitch the short ends together using the same process.

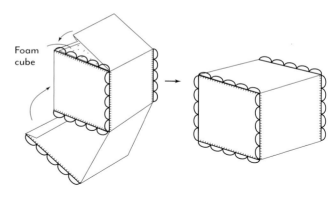

Foam
cube

EDGING MOTIFS

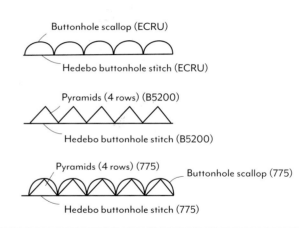

Buttonhole scallop (ECRU)

Hedebo buttonhole stitch (ECRU)

Pyramids (4 rows) (B5200)

Hedebo buttonhole stitch (B5200)

Pyramids (4 rows) (775)   Buttonhole scallop (775)

Hedebo buttonhole stitch (775)

Needle Book

Shown on page 34

MATERIALS

> Linen banding: 28 count in white
  – 13½ x 3⅛ in (34 x 8 cm)
> Thread: DMC coton a broder in
unbleached white (ECRU)
  – #16: 1 skein
> One ⅜ in (1 cm) diameter button
> 2¾ in (7 cm) square of beige wool
felt
> Cotton or polyester fiberfill

FINISHED SIZE

3⅛ x 3⅛ in (8 x 8 cm) when closed

INSTRUCTIONS

1. Fold the linen banding in half, aligning the short ends. Starting from the fold, hand stitch the two layers together for 3⅛ in (8 cm) along the top and bottom.

2. Stuff the 3⅛ in (8 cm) sewn area with fiberfill.

3. Sew a vertical seam down the center of the needle book to create the spine. Finish sewing the linen banding together for the remaining 3⅛ in (8 cm) along the top and bottom.

4. Fold and press the short ends over ⅜ in (1 cm) to the wrong side. Hand stitch the layers together, then sew the needlelace edging as noted in the diagram.

5. Hand stitch the felt in place along one side.

6. Fold the needle book in half along the spine created in step 3. Sew a button to the outside following the placement noted in the diagram.

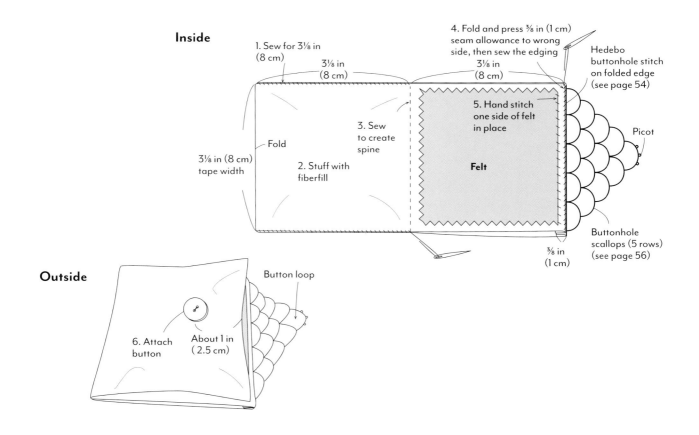

Inside

1. Sew for 3⅛ in (8 cm)

3⅛ in (8 cm)

4. Fold and press ⅜ in (1 cm) seam allowance to wrong side, then sew the edging

3⅛ in (8 cm)

Hedebo buttonhole stitch on folded edge (see page 54)

Fold

3. Sew to create spine

5. Hand stitch one side of felt in place

Felt

Picot

3⅛ in (8 cm) tape width

2. Stuff with fiberfill

Buttonhole scallops (5 rows) (see page 56)

⅜ in (1 cm)

Outside

Button loop

6. Attach button

About 1 in (2.5 cm)

Pincushion

Shown on page 35

MATERIALS

> Linen fabric: 55 count in unbleached white
  – 11¾ x 11¾ in (30 x 30 cm)
> Thread: DMC coton a broder in off-white (BLANC)
  – #30: 1 skein
> Linen fabric: Finely woven fabric in beige
  – 6¾ x 11 in (17 x 28 cm)
> 3½ in (9 cm) diameter cardboard circle
> Cotton or polyester fiberfill
> Small dish or jar with 4¼ in (11 cm) diameter

FINISHED SIZE

About 4½ x 4½ in (11.5 x 11.5 cm)

FULL-SIZE TEMPLATE

Pattern Sheet A

INSTRUCTIONS

1. Use the template on Pattern Sheet A and the Stitch Guide on page 153 to trace the cutting lines and embroidery design onto the center of the unbleached white linen fabric. Embroider as noted, except the edging. Trim into shape along the cutting lines (which include seam allowance). Fold and press the seam allowance over ⅜ in (1 cm) to the wrong side, clipping the curves where necessary. Complete the needlelace edging as noted in the Stitch Guide.

2. Cut a 6¾ in (17 cm) diameter circle of beige linen fabric. Mark a 4¼ in (11 cm) diameter circle for the finishing line, then sew running stitch ⅜ in (1 cm) outside the circle, leaving long thread tails.

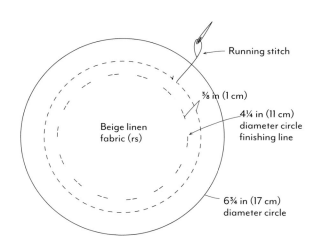

Running stitch

⅜ in (1 cm)

4¼ in (11 cm) diameter circle finishing line

Beige linen fabric (rs)

6¾ in (17 cm) diameter circle

3. Stuff with fiberfill and insert the cardboard circle, then pull the thread tails to gather the fabric around the cardboard. Take a few long stitches across the bottom to secure the fabric in place.

Cross-Section View

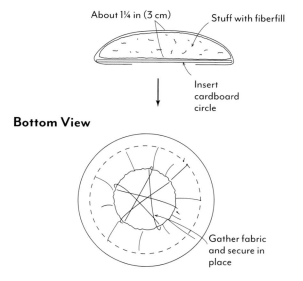

About 1¼ in (3 cm)

Stuff with fiberfill

Insert cardboard circle

Bottom View

Gather fabric and secure in place

4. Cut a 4¼ in (11 cm) diameter circle of beige linen fabric. Fold and press the seam allowance over ⅜ in (1 cm) to the wrong side. Hand stitch to the bottom.

5. Insert the pincushion into the dish. Position the embroidered work from step 1 on top and attach it to the base with discreet stitches at the inner points.

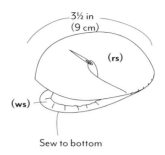

STITCH GUIDE

Use this to trace the embroidery design onto the fabric and to stitch. Use the template on Pattern Sheet A to mark the cutting lines and trim into shape.

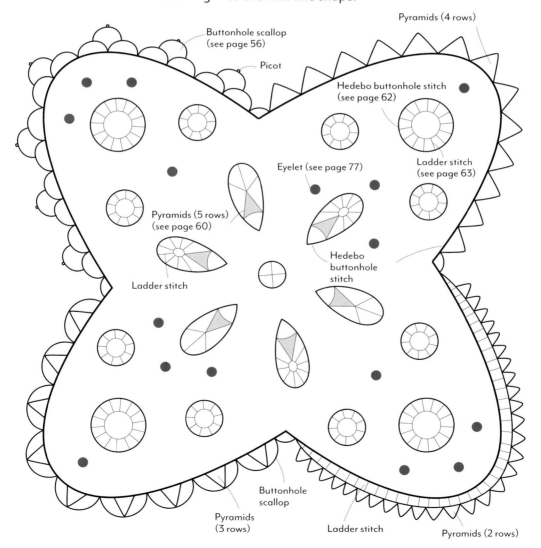

Basic Embroidery Stitches

Running Stitch

*For double running stitch, sew another line of running stitch between the first line of running stitches.

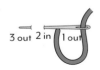 

3 out 2 in 1 out

3

Repeat 2 to 3

Stem Stitch

Make a thicker line by overlapping the stitches further.

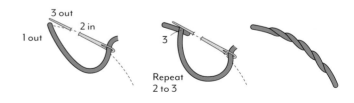

3 out 2 in

1 out

3

Repeat 2 to 3

Coral Stitch

3 out 2 in

1 out

Repeat 2 to 3

Straight Stitch

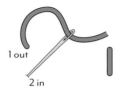

1 out

2 in

Lazy Daisy Stitch

3 out

4 in

1 out 2 in

Chain Stitch

3 2

1

3

Repeat 2 to 3

Satin Stitch

Start from the widest part of the shape to fill one half, then go back and fill the second half.

Out In

Satin Stitch with Padding

Work a layer of straight or chain stitches underneath the satin stitches to add thickness and height.

Open Chain Stitch

3 out 1 out

2 in

Repeat 2 to 3

Anchor two points
at the end

Buttonhole Stitch

2 in

3 out

1 out

3

Repeat 2 to 3

This stitch can be worked in
either direction.

French Knot Stitch

The knot size changes depending on the number of wraps.

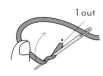

1 out

2

1 out

2 in
Pull
thread
through

Bullion Stitch

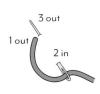 

3 out

1 out

2 in

Pull the needle through
as you gently hold the
wraps

3

2

2

4 in

Chevron Stitch

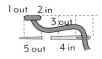   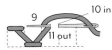 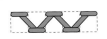

1 out 2 in

3 out

5 out 4 in

7 out

5

6 in

9 out 8 in

7

9

10 in

11 out

Repeat 4 to 11

Stitch Index